KT-473-964

Ethical
Dimensions
of
Leadership

Sage Series in Business Ethics

Series Editor: Robert A. Giacalone
The E. Claiborne Robins School of Business
University of Richmond

Editorial Board

Norman Bowie
University of Minnesota

F. Neil Brady
Brigham Young University

Steve Brenner
University of Portland

Rogene Bucholz
Loyola University–New Orleans

Archie Carroll
University of Georgia

Guido Corbetta
SDA Bocconi

Jerry Ferris
University of Illinois, Urbana-Champaign

Clive Fletcher
University of London

Donnelson Forsyth
Virginia Commonwealth University

Ed Gray
Loyola Marymount University

Jerald Greenberg
Ohio State University

Robert Hay
University of Arkansas

M. David Hoch
University of Southwestern Louisiana

John Kilpatrick
Idaho State University

Jeanne Liedtka
University of Virginia

Alex Michalos
University of Guelph, Canada

Dennis Moberg
Santa Clara University

Chimezie Obsigweh
Norfolk State University

Jean Pasquero
University of Quebec at Montreal

Stephen L. Payne
Eastern Illinois University

Barry Posner
Santa Clara University

Joanne Preston
Pepperdine University

Paul Rosenfeld
Navy Personnel Research & Development Center

James Schweikart
University of Richmond

Linda Trevino
Pennsylvania State University

Henk J. L. van Luijk
The Netherland School of Business

Scott Vitell
University of Mississippi

Donna Wood
University of Pittsburgh

Dan Worrell
Appalachian State University

Rabindra N. Kanungo
Manuel Mendonca

Ethical
Dimensions
of
Leadership

SSBE
Sage Series in Business Ethics

SAGE Publications
International Educational and Professional Publisher
Thousand Oaks   London   New Delhi

Copyright © 1996 by Sage Publications, Inc.

All rights reserved. No part of this book may be reproduced or utilized in any form or by any means, electronic or mechanical, including photocopying, recording, or by any information storage and retrieval system, without permission in writing from the publisher.

For information address:

SAGE Publications, Inc.
2455 Teller Road
Thousand Oaks, California 91320
E-mail: order@sagepub.com

SAGE Publications Ltd.
6 Bonhill Street
London EC2A 4PU
United Kingdom

SAGE Publications India Pvt. Ltd.
M-32 Market
Greater Kailash I
New Delhi 110 048 India

Printed in the United States of America

Library of Congress Cataloging-in-Publication Data

Kanungo, Rabindra Nath.
    Ethical dimensions of leadership / by Rabindra N. Kanungo,
Manuel Mendonca.
        p.   cm. — (Sage series in business ethics)
    Includes bibliographical references and indexes.
    ISBN 0-8039-5787-4 (cloth: alk. paper). — ISBN 0-8039-5788-2
(pbk.: alk. paper)
    1. Business ethics.   2. Leadership—Moral and ethical aspects.
3. Industrial management—Moral and ethical aspects.   I. Mendonca,
Manuel.   II. Title.   III. Series.
    HF5387.K35   1996
    174′.4—dc20   95-35992

This book is printed on acid-free paper.

96 97 98 99 10 9 8 7 6 5 4 3 2 1

Production Editor: Tricia K. Bennett   Typesetter: Christina Hill

To our ancestors who valued wisdom over intellect

For if there be no mind
Debating good and ill,
And if religion send
No challenge to the will,
If only greed be there
For some material feast,
How draw a line between
The man-beast and the beast?

—*The Panchantantra* (translated from Sanskrit
by A. W. Ryder, Bombay: JAICO, 1959, p. 7)

Have they made thee ruler?
be not lifted up: be among them as one of them.
Have care of them, and so sit down,
and when thou hast acquitted thyself of all thy charge,
take thy place:
That thou mayst rejoice for them,
and receive a crown as an ornament of grace,
and get the honour of the contribution.

—*Ecclesiasticus 32: 1-3*
(*The Holy Bible,* Douay-Rheims version,
Baltimore: John Murphy, 1899)

Contents

Preface

"Is there a crisis in business ethics?" Although the responses to this question might vary, there seems to be a consensus in contemporary North American society that there is at least an ethical malaise, if not a full-blown ethical crisis. A malaise means that the body is experiencing discomfort, but not signs of a specific disease. In a crisis, the disease has appeared, creating a situation of imminent danger. Nevertheless, it is imprudent to ignore a malaise because it is only a matter of time before it worsens. Because individuals, whether acting alone or collectively as organizational members, hold values such as justice, honesty, trustworthiness, and loyalty in high regard, it will not be long before the ethical malaise in an organization operating in an amoral environment becomes an ethical crisis.

Have we reached this turning point, this moment of danger? Almost no day seems to go by without some media exposure of unethical behavior of organizational leaders or exhortations about the need for ethics in business and public life. There is a greater public perception today that profits, regardless of any other consideration, are the major driving force of business and that even unethical means seem to be justified in the relentless pursuit of profit. Business education also seems to be affected by an ethical malaise. As we see from the examples cited in the book, an unusually strong emphasis on self-centeredness seems to characterize the values of business students.

It is, therefore, not surprising that society demands and expects greater accountability from business organizations and business schools. The leadership of these organizations bears the primary responsibility to respond to these demands. The beliefs and values, the vision, and above all, the actions of the leader set the ethical tone and standards for the organization. The ethical behavior of organizational members is inspired by the leader in much the same way that the caboose, the boxcar, the cattle car, and so on move on the established rails by the pulling power of the engine. It is this fundamentally crucial role of the leader that has prompted the writing of this book. It proposes that one's understanding of leadership is severely incomplete, if not distorted, if one does not also consider the ethics or morality of leadership.

For far too long, the literature on leadership, especially business leadership, has neglected the ethical issues by its focus only on approaches and strategies that emphasize self-centered, individualistic concerns. There seems to be a schizophrenic attitude to moral and ethical values. In our private lives, we might be quite comfortable with moral ideals influencing our behavior. But, for some strange reason, the influence of these same ideals does not seem to carry over to behavior in the workplace. Instead, the implicit expectations or norms in the workplace seem to be influenced by expediency or pragmatism in order to attain the organization's economic objectives. The approach to the book assumes that "unity of life" is a basic principle that ought to govern human behavior. Consequently, individuals who aspire to leadership cannot expect to live separate lives with different, and often contradictory, sets of values for each. The book examines the various modal orientations of leadership and demonstrates that true, effective leadership is one in which the leader's behavior and the exercise of the leadership influence process are consistent with ethical and moral values. To such a leader, honesty, for instance, is not a matter of "policy" but of virtue. The book, therefore, argues for an end to the traditional separation of personal and public morality. It also argues that the ethics of leadership is consistent with the spirituality of the different religious traditions. Such spirituality can provide the leader with the inner strength and sustenance to be true to the moral demands that are made in the exercise of leadership.

We believe that the book will serve the needs of business educational programs, business consultants, and researchers. The relatively exhaustive and integrated conceptual treatment of the leadership phenomenon, consistent with ethical and moral values, will greatly enhance leadership courses in business schools or executive development programs. It is also of interest to those in courses in business ethics, organizational behavior, and managerial skills development. The inclusion of the cultural contingencies in leadership, in the context of non-Western sociocultural environments, extends its suitability and usefulness for courses in international business and international management. The practical orientation, in addition to the conceptual framework, offers practitioners and consultants practical strategies for effective leadership, such as empowerment, together with suggestions of how leaders can prepare for ethical leadership. These strategies and suggestions can aid the practitioner or consultant who is invariably called on to prescribe different forms of interventions to increase organizational effectiveness. Finally, the review of the literature, the conceptual models, and the issues and questions that are identified are intended to prompt further research and study into the morality of leadership.

Rabindra N. Kanungo
Manuel Mendonca

Introduction and Overview

It would be a truism to state that organizations have been in existence for as long as there have been human beings. The social characteristics and needs of a human being are an inherent and inextricable element of human nature, which creates the necessity for organizations. Numerous organizations can be found in human society, each specializing in providing a variety of goods and services to promote the well-being of its members. Every society, regardless of the state of its development, has family, educational, religious, economic, and political institutions that serve to address the varied needs of its members.

The basic feature of these organizations and their constituent elements is people with a set of shared beliefs and values and a common purpose. They form an organization to achieve, consistent with their beliefs and values, this common purpose that they see to be beneficial to themselves and to the society at large. The organizations, as we know them today, are vastly different than those from the beginning of human existence. However, human beings seem to have realized early on that organizations are inevitable for the very survival of their species if they are to cope successfully with the demands of the environment. Organizations serve human beings well. The family, the school, religious institutions—all play a pivotal role in the development of the human being from a helpless infant to an independent, mature, and morally responsible adult. The economic and political institutions contribute to such development through programs and laws designed to sustain a self-supporting and self-governing society.

▧ THE NEED FOR LEADERSHIP IN ORGANIZATIONS

A closer analysis of organizations would reveal that these are more than a random assembly of people, albeit with a common purpose. Organizations have a structure. In fact, it is precisely because of the desire to achieve this purpose efficiently and effectively that organizational members assume or are assigned different tasks, roles, and status levels in the organization. Stated differently, organizational structures imply that there are leaders and followers. The leaders are expected to provide direction, exercise control, and generally execute such functions that are necessary to achieve the organization's objectives. In successful organizations, true leadership behavior—in the sense of leading others—is more than routine maintenance activities such as allocating resources, monitoring and directing employees, and building cohesion in the work group. True leadership involves moving followers toward the realization of the vision that the leader has formulated to fulfill the organization's mission. Clearly, organizations need leadership. Without a leader, the organization is much like a rudderless ship—adrift in a turbulent environment. For this reason, the study of leadership, its modal orientations and processes, is an instructive and fruitful endeavor for students of organizations and management practitioners.

▧ THE NEED FOR ETHICS IN LEADERSHIP

However, one might legitimately question the need for the study of ethics in leadership. If we think about it, the greatest number of organizations that exist are in the business and government sectors, which, it might be argued, really are or should be unconcerned with ethics or morality. The argument might be that ethics and morality are or ought to be the exclusive preserve of religious and, possibly, educational organizations. When morality intrudes into the business organization, it has the potential of diverting business leaders from the organization's primary objectives and, as a result, causing it to be inefficient and to deprive stockholders of their due returns. Surely, the founder did not start the business to promote morality but rather to earn a profit and create wealth. Similar questions can also be raised about the role of ethics in nonbusiness or not-for-profit organizations, including the government—the largest of all organizations in the country.

The beginnings of a response to these questions can be traced to Aristotle's *Politics.* In it, Aristotle observed that the state comes into being to provide law and order but continues for the sake of good law, good order, and noble actions. In a similar vein, the raison d'être of human organizations—their structure and mechanisms, norms and activity—is to support some "good" and be in accord with the "highest excellence." As Peter Drucker (1968) observed:

> What is most important is that management realize that it must consider the impact of every business policy and business action upon society. It has to consider whether the action is likely to promote the public good, to advance the basic beliefs of our society, to contribute to its stability, strength and harmony. (p. 461)

It is the recognition of this responsibility that has led several large corporations to formulate codes of ethics for their organizations (Berenbeim, 1987).

All organizational members bear the responsibility to ensure that organizational objectives are achieved in a manner that is consistent with these ideals and serve their own welfare as well as the larger interests of society. However, the primary duty and responsibility for providing the proper direction and the high standards of performance rest chiefly with the organizational leader. He or she is indeed the soul of the organization. The leader's vision inspires and articulates the organization's mission; provides the basis for the organization's objectives and goals; communicates the beliefs and values that influence and shape the organization's culture and behavioral norms; and lays the foundation for organizational strategies, policies, and procedures. The organization's mission statement and policies—however noble, well-crafted, and articulated— are absolutely futile if the leader's actions and behavior are inconsistent with these statements.

There is an increasing realization today that business leaders need to become more responsible, not just to their stockholders but also to their other stakeholders—consumers, employees, suppliers, the government, and local communities. Although no one will deny that a business must be profitable, the sole preoccupation with profit to the exclusion or neglect of other considerations is no longer acceptable. Profits—once the be-all and end-all of business—are now viewed as a means to serve the larger interests of society, which, in effect, implies that business decisions should be based on high standards of both economic and ethical performance. A survey of human resource executives found that 67% of the respondents observed that ethics would be more important for organizations in the future (Halcrow, 1987).

In the popular media as well as in academic journals, we see much public interest in the proposition that business and other organizational leaders need to be more sensitive to their responsibilities to all their stakeholders. Along with the impressive breakthroughs in technology providing new and better products and services, the improved communications transforming the world into a global village, the greater sense of participation in public life, and generally the higher standard of living, we witness events and developments in the area of public and private morality that make us question whether the much-hailed economic and social progress in the developed countries is, indeed, "progress" and, if so, if it is worthwhile.

We see reports of paying bribes to government officials, insider trading, marketing of adulterated apple juice, and lack of moral probity and integrity among some business leaders, professionals, and members of the clergy. We see environmental pollution; hemophiliacs contracting the AIDS virus because some government officials knowingly allowed the use of contaminated blood; and, in many otherwise prosperous and affluent cities, we see an increase in numbers of homeless people and lengthening lines at the foodbanks. We also hear reports of a glue that contains a nauseous substance to discourage "sniffing" by youngsters when it is manufactured for the North American market, but, to reduce costs, this substance is left out when it is manufactured for markets in South America even though the same potential for harm exists for youngsters in those markets. Many employees who are fortunate enough to have jobs find that work not only does not provide an opportunity for growth and self-fulfillment, but it also is a source of much anxiety and insecurity because of employees' apprehension that they might be the next to be sacrificed on the altar of short-term objectives—quarterly profits, market share, gross sales, or return on investment.

It is, indeed, unfortunate that business organizations have been subjected to so much criticism. We owe a great deal to the business enterprise. It provides us with the products and services we need and with the opportunities to cultivate and make use of our talents, knowledge, and abilities. It also contributes to the economy, and the living standards we enjoy would be unthinkable without the contemporary business organization. The many important advancements in medicine, education, and technology have resulted from the efforts or support of business corporations. And yet the preceding litany of woes has probably provoked the observation that "our people have lost faith in the basic values of our economic society, and that we need a spiritual rebirth in industrial leadership. . . . Can it be that our *god of production has feet of clay?* Does industry need a new religion—or at least a better one than it has had?" (Ohmann, 1989, p. 59). A proper reflection and analysis of this question would suggest that, as an entity, the business corporation is incapable of doing good or evil in society. Such results must be directly and entirely attributed to the unethical behavior of individuals—workers or managers of the corporation.

For this reason, there is a growing awareness that ethical principles ought to govern the decisions of our leaders, that schools ought to regard character formation as the core element of their mission. This would seem to be particularly necessary in the case of management education. Based on a review of theoretical and empirical research, Daboub, Rasheed, Priem, and Gray (1995) have developed a model that suggests the relationship between the characteristics of the organization's top management team and corporate criminal activity. The model postulates that, other things being equal, the more formal education in management (e.g., an MBA) that members of top management possess, the higher the chances of corporate criminal activity. The model clearly suggests that management educators do not seem to provide adequate training and formation in business ethics. As Walton (1988) has observed, "Teachers cannot ignore what leaders cannot do without" (p. 7). Similar sentiments are echoed by Andrews (1989), when he suggests that "the problem of corporate ethics has three aspects: the development of the executive as a moral person; the influence of the corporation as a moral environment; and the actions needed to map a high road to economic and ethical performance—and to mount guardrails to keep corporate wayfarers on track" (p. 99).

It is not enough that managers are intelligent, industrious, and competent in their technical specialty because studies have shown that, despite these desirable qualities, they might be ineffective "because they are perceived as arrogant, vindictive, untrustworthy, selfish, emotional, compulsive, over-controlling, insensitive, [and] abrasive" (Hogan, Curphy, & Hogan, 1994, p. 499). In addition to the individual's ethical qualities, the organization's moral environment is equally important. It is most unlikely that the unethical practices cited previously are entirely those of the individual "rogue" employee. An unethical practice generally involves "the tacit, if not explicit, cooperation of others and reflects the values, attitudes, beliefs, language, and behavioral patterns that define an organization's operating culture" (Paine, 1994, p. 106).

The quality of life and the very survival of a human society depend on the moral caliber of its members. However, the moral caliber of members is largely determined by people in leadership positions. The manner in which leaders function in these positions of influence can directly contribute to the strengthening or the deterioration of the moral fiber of society. The lives of Socrates, Buddha, Mohammed, Lao-Tzu, Gandhi—to name a few—attest to their salutary influence in their own day, as well as for all time. On the other hand, the recent case of senior government officials in France who knowingly permitted the use of contaminated blood, resulting in the deaths of several hundred hemophiliacs, strikingly illustrates the harm that a few can inflict on individuals and society. When people in leadership positions compromise their moral values, they do more than physical harm. Their callous neglect or compromise of moral values also contributes to creating an atmosphere of moral cynicism that, like a cancer, corrodes the moral health of society.

The role of a leader has always carried with it grave and onerous responsibilities. In our time, the burden of this role poses rather unique and formidable challenges because of the fundamental shift in societal norms and values. We refer specifically to "economic imperialism" (Hirsch, 1976; Schwartz, 1986) and the cult of "self-worship" (Vitz, 1994), which is so pervasive in North America. According to Schwartz (1990), economic imperialism is "the spread of economic calculations of *interest* to domains that were once regarded as noneconomic" (p. 13). For example, education has come to be viewed by students as an economic investment, and, therefore, students approach it almost entirely based on its potential to generate salary dollars. As a result, the sole criterion to evaluate education is the earning capacity it has bestowed on the students. In the process, the fundamental purpose of and reason for education—that is, the search for truth—is forgotten. Therefore, one should not be surprised at the comment that Harvard Business School graduates seem to think that there is nothing more to life than money, self-interest, fame, and power (Etzioni, 1989). Nor should one be surprised at the findings that 40% to 90% of university students admit to cheating and that it is acceptable so long as one does not get caught (Watson, 1991).

The cult of self-worship is based on the assumption that "reward for the self (i.e., egoism) is the only functional ethical principle" (Vitz, 1994, p. xi). Drawing on modern psychological theories of human motivation and personality, whether intended to or not by the theorists, the cult of self-worship or self-theory has spawned a plethora of techniques, programs, and self-help books designed to make people "feel good about themselves." Underlying these approaches is the emphasis on the rights of individuals to self-actualization and fulfillment of their potential in any form or manner they choose without much regard or concern to one's duties and obligations to others. A striking example of this narcissistic self-love is captured in the advice to teachers that they should neither grade their students nor label or categorize them. Instead, they should make them feel good about themselves (Kramer, 1991). This focus on self is an "extreme expression of individualistic psychology first created by a frontier society and now supported and corrupted by consumerism. Today it is reinforced by educators who gratify the vanity of even our youngest children with repetitive mantras like: *The most important person in the whole wide world is you, and you hardly even know you!*" (Vitz, 1994, p. 21).

On this issue of self-love, the observation of Donald Campbell (1975), a social psychologist and a former president of the American Psychological Association, is most pertinent:

> There is in psychology today a general background assumption that the human impulses provided by biological evolution are right and optimal, both individually and socially, and that repressive or inhibitory moral traditions are wrong. This assumption may now be regarded as scientifically wrong. Psychology, in propagating this background perspective in its teaching of perhaps 80 or 90 percent of college undergraduates, and increasing proportions of high school and elementary school pupils, helps to undermine the retention of what may be extremely valuable social-evolutionary systems which we do not fully understand. (pp. 1120-1121)

The preceding sampling of contemporary events and ideas suggests the absolute need for moral leadership in organizations and in society. It is in the context of such need that we discuss the phenomenon of leadership and its ethical dimensions because, for better or for worse, organizational leaders are ultimately and unquestionably the fundamental agents of change.

▧ AN OVERVIEW OF THE BOOK

We first begin with a historical perspective on leadership theory and research (Chapter 2). We will explore the diversity of approaches and empirical findings that have led some to observe that there is a crisis in leadership research. In an effort to address this issue of the lack of a unifying comprehensive theoretical framework, the chapter identifies the modal orientations of leadership theory and research on essentially three aspects: leader role behavior, contingencies of leadership effectiveness, and the leader-follower influence process. It then assesses the limitations of existing theoretical paradigms and examines the emerging trends in leadership theory and research. The chapter concludes with a development of a conceptual framework of charismatic or transformational leadership, which we believe best responds to the needs of organizations in a highly turbulent environment and in the context of increasing globalization of business and interdependence among nations.

Chapter 3 examines the motivational basis of leadership. It examines the critical needs that serve as motives for leader behavior—needs such as affiliation, achievement, and power. These motives are considered within the overarching framework of altruism, which provides the ethical justification of leader behavior. For this purpose, the chapter discusses the nature of altruism as a motivational construct, the morality underlying altruism, and the resulting ethical implications for leadership and the norms for leader behavior. The influence processes that characterize the leader-follower relationship are discussed in Chapter 4. More specifically, this chapter discusses the transactional and transformational influence processes and the related strategic options available to the leader. The nature of the strategies involved in each process and their effects on the leader-follower interactions are examined together with their ethical implications. The discussion makes the point that the influence process that is consistent with ethical principles is the one that brings about the transformation of both the leader and the followers.

The thrust of the preceding chapters is to develop the idea that the expertise and experience, styles and impression management, and other techniques and accoutrements of a leader are effective only to the extent that these are imbued with sound ethical principles. Therefore, in Chapter 5, the focus is on what leaders can do to prepare themselves to function as ethical leaders. It begins with a discussion of the obstacles to altruism in organizations and the reasons why it is needed in organizations. In business management, the objective of the study of ethics has traditionally been the development of analytical and decision-making skills through exercises in resolving ethical dilemmas and quandaries. Such an approach to the study of ethics might be seen by the students more as a purely intellectual exercise rather than as a means to the development of moral insights and the formation of character through the practice of human and moral virtues. As a result, ethics has been treated as distinct and separate from spirituality. The discussion in the chapter demonstrates that spirituality is an integral part of ethics. It provides sustenance to the leader's efforts to develop a moral character possessed of inner strength and resourcefulness, and to create a moral environment in the organization. It also explores some of the sources that spiritual sages of all time recommend that leaders draw on for the needed spiritual strength, solace, and inspiration to exercise the leadership that is uplifting to themselves and their followers.

The concluding chapter examines the cultural contingencies in leadership and pancultural moral values. This issue is pertinent and crucial in the context of the increasing globalization of business and the interdependence among nations. It highlights the importance of sociocultural variables that can influence the behavior of leaders and followers, as well as the nature of the leader-follower relationship. It also examines the ethical implications of leadership motivation and influence processes as viewed from different cultural perspectives—whether societal cultures make ethical considerations more or less salient and relevant depending on the moral values inherent in them.

Leadership Theory and Research:
Modal Orientations and Emerging Trends

L eaders have been celebrated in folklore, art, music, opera, and literature, both mythical and historical; statues, triumphal arches, mausoleums, and magnificent edifices have been built to honor them; cities, ships, aircraft, and even babies have been named after them. They have been blessed and cursed, but to the bewilderment and frustration of scholars, they have not been understood: Like the early morning mist soon dispelled by the rising sun, the leadership phenomenon seems to elude them. The examination of leadership as a group and organizational phenomenon has been the focus of both theoretical and empirical analysis for more than a half century (Bass, 1990a; Bennis & Nanus, 1985; Burns, 1978; Hollander, 1978).

Literally thousands of articles, papers, and books on the topic have examined and probed the leadership phenomenon from every conceivable angle. Yet, like any complex social psychological phenomenon, our understanding remains incomplete in spite of the decades of research. Commenting on the state of our knowledge in 1959, Bennis wrote:

> Of all the hazy and confounding areas in social psychology, leadership theory undoubtedly contends for top nomination. And, ironically, probably more has been written and less known about leadership than about any other topic in the behavioral sciences. Always, it seems the concept of leadership eludes us or turns up in another form to taunt us again with its slipperiness and complexity. (pp. 259-260)

More than three decades after Bennis's assessment, the situation has not changed much. In a recent comment on the "leadership mystique," Kets de Vries (1994) observed:

> As far as leadership studies go, it seems that more and more has been studied about less and less, to end up ironically with a group of researchers studying everything about nothing. It prompted one wit to say recently that reading the current world literature on leadership is rather like going through the Parisian telephone directory while trying to read it in Chinese! (p. 73)

Social scientists such as political scientists (e.g., Burns, 1978; Wilner, 1984), sociologists (e.g., Bradley, 1987; Roberts, 1985), organization theorists (e.g., Nadler & Tushman, 1990; Pfeffer, 1977), psychoanalysts (e.g., Kets de Vries, 1994; Zaleznik, 1990), and psychologists (e.g., Bass, 1990a; Hollander & Offermann, 1990) have contributed to the enigmatic nature of the leadership phenomenon by proposing various analytical frameworks and focusing on different content and process aspects of leadership in a wide range of contexts. Very often, these multidisciplinary approaches have spoken different languages that are specific to their own disciplines and sometimes unintelligible to those of the other disciplines. These approaches have also adopted levels of analyses as diverse as micro and macro, individual and interactional, process and structure to explain the constructs and processes related to the phenomenon.

The resulting disparate, incomparable analytical treatments (see, e.g., Bryman, 1986; Hunt, Baliga, Dachler, & Schriesheim, 1988; Yukl, 1989) and empirical attempts have provided conflicting evidence on the role of leadership in organizational and group performance, which have obscured rather than facilitated our understanding of the phenomenon. One is reminded of a party game in which blindfolded participants are asked to describe a model of an elephant only by touching it. The participants describe the elephant in terms of the part they are able to touch. So some say it is a firm, round cylinder when they touch the leg, or a flexible, hairy wand when they get hold of the tail, or a large, soft flap when they come to the ear. None is able to comprehend the elephant in its entirety. Peter Dorfman (1994) has used an equally telling metaphor to describe the situation: "If we can think of leadership research flowing as a stream, it flows in a meandering, intertwining, and constantly shifting manner" (p. 4).

This state of affairs in leadership research has created considerable difficulty for scholars at both the conceptual and empirical levels of study. At the conceptual level, there is the difficulty of developing integrative and reasonably comprehensive frameworks to understand the leadership phenomenon. At the empirical level, the ambiguity of research findings has led some to even question the usefulness of research endeavors in the leadership area. Researchers in both psychology and management (Fiedler & Chemers, 1974; House, 1988a; Kerr & Jermier, 1978; Pfeffer, 1977) have debated the issue of what precisely are the critical properties and processes of the leadership phenomenon. They have also tried to establish the empirical validity of the leadership construct by asking whether leadership does or does not make a difference in explaining and predicting the success or failure of groups and organizations. Such attempts have neither produced a unifying and comprehensive theoretical framework (Bryman, 1986) nor have they succeeded to establish empirically an unequivocal link between leadership and organizational and group performance (Thomas, 1988). Hence, we have several splinter theories of leadership and numerous empirical studies within each advocacy camp, which have led many to describe this state of affairs as a "crisis in leadership research" (Hunt et al., 1988, p. 243).

One should not infer from the preceding discussion that past research explorations of the leadership phenomenon have been totally fruitless. Likewise, it would be erroneous and unwise to infer that research pursuits in the area should be given up because of the existing crisis or because of the complex and enigmatic nature of the phenomenon. Rather, the phenomenal complexity and the elusive character of the leadership construct must be seen as a problem whose resolution would greatly enrich our knowledge. In essence, it is a challenge for the social scientist whose major task is to describe and unravel the mysteries underlying such social phenomena. This is particularly true for social and organizational psychologists whose objective is to study behavioral processes in groups and organizations because leadership—its behaviors and processes—forms an essential, if not the key, element of group and organizational processes.

Our purpose here is not to get entangled in the controversy of whether it is feasible or even worthwhile to study the leadership phenomenon that has eluded us thus far. We believe that "the romance of leadership" in groups and organizations and among both researchers and management practitioners is too strong to deny its legitimate status as a behavioral phenomenon to be studied scientifically (Hogan et al., 1994; House, 1988a; Meindl, Ehrlich, & Dukerich, 1985). We also agree with House's (1988a) assertion that critics of leadership research often "misrepresent the current state of leadership knowledge" and "underestimate the amount of knowledge produced to date" (p. 248).

Although we recognize the importance of existing knowledge and the need to continue scientific research on leadership to better understand the phenomenon, we do not intend to present here an exhaustive review of the enormous psychological literature on the topic. Such reviews exist elsewhere (e.g., Bass, 1990a; Yukl, 1989). Rather, the purpose of this chapter is to enhance our understanding of the leadership phenomenon by seeking answers to questions such as: What have we learned from the past leadership debates in the psychological literature? On which issues is there most agreement among researchers? What ought to be the future direction of leadership research in the field of organizational behavior? The research in leadership has encompassed many disciplines, such as anthropology, sociology, and political science. Our focus, however, will be restricted to leadership from the point of view of social and organizational psychology.

Thus, our objective is fourfold: first, to identify some basic assumptions underlying leadership theory and research; second, to indicate the modal orientations in leadership paradigms reflected in the writings of social and organizational psychologists; third, to assess the limitations of the dominant leadership paradigms; and fourth, to suggest a shift of focus from the study of the conventional leadership parameters to the study of parameters largely ignored so far by behavioral scientists. This fourfold analysis will provide the foundation for a focus on those aspects of leadership that have ethical implications, and these issues will be addressed, chiefly, in Chapters 3 and 4.

◩ BASIC ASSUMPTIONS UNDERLYING LEADERSHIP THEORY AND RESEARCH

All volitional acts in response to an environment are guided by our assumptions about the nature of that environment. The acts of a researcher are no exception. The theoretical frameworks and investigative strategies that researchers adopt when they explore a behavioral phenomenon are to a large extent directed by their assumptions about the nature of that phenomenon. In fact, the controversies and misunderstandings among researchers can often be traced to the failure to recognize that differences exist in respect to the implicit assumptions adopted in their studies, hence, the need to be as explicit as possible about one's assumptions. For this reason, as we attempt to identify the modal orientations in leadership research, we first begin by explicitly stating a set of commonly held assumptions about the leadership phenomenon among social and organizational psychologists.

First, researchers in social and organizational psychology have come to accept leadership as an organizational or group phenomenon. The phenomenon is observed as a *set of role behaviors* performed by an individual when there is a need to influence and coordinate the activities of group or organizational members toward the achievement of a common goal. This individual is called the leader, and the focus on behaviors can be said to be the behavioral approach to leadership. Before the behavioral approach, leadership was viewed in terms of the "great man" or "traits" theory of leadership, which essentially proposed that the success of a leader is to be attributed solely to his or her personality and physical traits or characteristics without regard to the situational context (Cowley, 1928).

Numerous studies failed to identify such traits and found it to be a much too simplistic explanation of the complex leadership phenomenon (Dorfman, 1994). Thus, instead of studying leadership as a cluster of stable personality traits, in isolation from their context, we today view leadership as a set of role behaviors by individuals in the context of the group or organization to which they belong. Thus, as Cartwright and Zander (1968) point out, "Leadership consists of such actions by group members as those which aid in setting group goals, moving the group toward its goals, improving the quality of interactions among the members, building cohesiveness of the group, and making resources available to the group" (p. 304).

From this description of leadership—as a set of role behaviors in a group context—follows the assumption that leadership is both a *relational* and an *attributional* phenomenon. The existence of a leader depends on the existence of one or more followers and the kind of status or power relationship that develops between them. However, leadership comes into being when followers perceive the leader's behavior in a certain way, accept the leader's influence attempts, and then attribute the leadership status to the individual. Without the followers' perceptions, acceptance, and attributions, the phenomenon would simply not exist.

Third, it is commonly assumed that while studying the phenomenon, one can reveal both its *contents* and its *processes*. The contents refer to the types of leader role behaviors, the attributes of leaders, followers, and situational contexts when the phenomenon is observed. The study of the content of leadership involves the identification of specific sets of leader role behaviors that serve to achieve the group's objectives by influencing the attitudes and behavior of group members. The study of leadership content also permits us to identify the properties of followers and situations, such as the task, the social climate, and so on, that facilitate or hinder the manifestation of the leadership phenomenon. By leadership processes we refer to the types of social influence processes that operate and the psychological dynamics underlying them. Thus, leadership implies the exercise of influence over others through the use of various bases of social power, reinforcers, tacts, and so on to elicit the group members' compliance with certain norms and their commitment necessary to achieve the group's objectives.

This distinction of content and process in leadership research leads to a further assumption. The assumption is that to understand leadership phenomenon, one must analyze the properties of the basic *leadership elements* and the major *relational processes.* The basic leadership elements are the leader, the followers, and the situational context. The major relational processes are the leader-follower influence process, the leader-context relational process, and the context-follower relational process (see Conger & Kanungo, 1988c, for this type of analysis of charismatic leadership).

This brings us to the final assumption. The role behaviors of a leader are intended to directly influence followers' attitudes and behavior within the group or organizational context. Thus, *leadership effectiveness* should be measured in terms of (a) the degree to which a leader promotes the instrumental attitudes and behavior for the achievement of group objectives; (b) the followers' satisfaction with the task and context within which they operate; and (c) the acceptance of the leader's influence, which is often manifested through the followers' emotional bond with the leader, by their attributions of favorable qualities to the leader, and by their compliance behavior and commitment attitudes and values. However, instead of these measures, leadership effectiveness is more often measured in terms of group or organizational productivity. As Yukl (1989) points out:

> The most commonly used measure of leader effectiveness is the extent to which the leader's group or organization performs its task successfully and attains its goals. In some cases, objective measures of performance or goal attainment are available, such as profit growth, profit margin, sales increase, market share, sales relative to targeted sales, return on investment, produc-

tivity, cost per unit or output, costs in relation to budgeted expenditures, and so on. (p. 6)

We do not believe these are appropriate measures of a leader's influence or effectiveness simply because these indexes of group-level or organization-level productivity, however objective these might be, depend not only on the followers' instrumental behavior but also on available environmental resources, technology, market condition, and so on, over which a leader has little control.

▨ MODAL ORIENTATIONS IN LEADERSHIP PARADIGMS

The modal orientation of past leadership research in both social and organizational psychology has been to address three specific issues related to the ways of viewing leadership and leadership effectiveness constructs, described in the previous section. A concern for the understanding of the "leadership" construct led to the first research issue of identifying *leader role behavior* in group contexts. A similar concern for understanding the nature of leadership effectiveness led to the second and third research issues. Specifically, the second research issue dealt with the task of identifying the *contingencies of leadership effectiveness* through the study of the interactions between the leader, the follower, and the situational context. The third issue focused on understanding the nature of leadership effectiveness by analyzing the underlying mechanisms of the *leader-follower influence process* itself. We shall now briefly discuss each of these three modal trends.

Leader Role Behavior

Early research studies aimed at identifying leadership role behavior by examining small formal and informal groups in both laboratory and field settings. These investigations (Bales & Slater, 1955; Cartwright & Zander, 1968; Fleishman, Harris, & Burtt, 1955; Halpin & Winer, 1952) converged on the thesis that leadership role behavior is functionally related to two broad group objectives: group maintenance and group task achievement. A group member, in an informal group, or an appointed leader, in a formal group, is perceived to be acting as a leader when he or she engages in activities that promote group maintenance and/or ensure task performance and goal achievement. Following in this vein, later studies of supervision and leadership in organizations (Yukl, 1989) identified two major leadership roles, a consideration or people orientation, also known as the social role, and an initiating structure or task orientation, also known as the task role.

The first role, consideration or people orientation, reflects the social-emotional leadership: "The degree to which the leader's behavior towards group members is characterized by mutual trust, development of good relations, sensitivity to the feelings of group members, and openness to their suggestions" (Andriessen & Drenth, 1984, p. 489). The second role, initiating structure in the group, reflects the task-oriented leadership: "The degree to which a leader is bent on defining and structuring the various tasks and roles of group members in order to attain group results" (Andriessen & Drenth, 1984, p. 489). This two-dimensional approach greatly influenced management practice as evidenced by the popularity of leadership training programs such as the management grid (Blake & Mouton, 1964), which sought to identify the managers' predominant orientation—whether it was a task or a social orientation.

Contingencies of Leadership Effectiveness

The second research issue—identification of conditions or contingencies of leadership effectiveness—has also been studied using small groups in both laboratory and field settings. Expanding on the earlier constructs of leader role behavior, Fiedler (1967) initiated the notion that a particular leader attribute was contingent on the situational context for its effectiveness. An example of such an attribute might be initiating structure versus consideration, or Fiedler's operational measures of low and high LPC—that is, "least preferred co-worker." In certain situations with certain types of tasks and follower attitudes, initiating structure would be more effective than consideration and vice versa. In a related approach, Kerr and Jermier (1978) identified two kinds of situational factors referred to as substitutes or neutralizers of leadership influence on subordinates. Their "substitutes for leadership" specify a set of characteristics of followers, tasks, and organizational contexts that reduces or nullifies the effects of relationship- and task-oriented leadership roles.

Building on the classic studies of autocratic and democratic leadership by Lewin and his associates (Lewin, Lippitt, & White, 1939; Lippitt & White, 1947), another stream of contingency theorists also emerged. These researchers explored the effects of autocratic, consultative, and participative leadership behavior on the effectiveness of a leader in achieving group objectives, whether these might be solely people oriented or task oriented. Their published findings in both the social psychological and organizational behavior literature (Coch & French, 1948; Likert, 1961; McGregor, 1960; Tannenbaum & Schmidt, 1958; Vroom & Yetton, 1973) suggested that the extent to which leaders involved followers in their decision making was a critical factor in leadership effectiveness. Using a continuum of styles from autocratic to consultative to participative, the models identified a style that was most appropriate to the characteristics of the situation—keeping in mind both the tasks and the followers.

Leader-Follower Influence Process

The third research issue delved into questions of how and why leaders become effective in influencing their followers. This issue examined the psychological mechanisms that explain the linkage between the leader's role behavior and the followers' compliance and commitment to achieving group or organizational objectives. These questions were explored from three different theoretical perspectives: (a) the bases of social power (Dahl, 1957; French & Raven, 1959), (b) the nature of social exchange (Blau, 1974; Hollander, 1979), and (c) the motivational dynamics (Evans, 1970; House, 1971; Luthans & Kreitner, 1975).

Exploring the reasons for leadership power and influence, Cartwright (1965) suggested that leadership effectiveness stems from followers' perception that leaders possess and control resources valued by followers. Control over such resources forms the bases of power (Dahl, 1957) of leaders. Most studies of leadership effectiveness using this perspective (e.g., Kanungo, 1977; Student, 1968), however, have used French and Raven's (1959) formulation of five kinds of resources that form the bases of social power: reward, coercive, legal, expert, and referent power bases. The first three bases of social power are often assumed to stem from one's formal authority position within a group or an organization. Hence, they are referred to as position power bases. The last two, expert and referent power bases, are considered to be residing in the leader's idiosyncratic ways of influencing followers. Hence, they are termed personal power or idiosyncratic power bases. The use of personal power by a leader has an incremental influence on followers (Katz & Kahn, 1978) over and above the influence that results from the use of the leader's position power. Such incremental influence on followers is reflected in the followers' performance beyond the organizationally prescribed performance expectations.

The second theoretical perspective used to explain leadership influence makes use of social exchange theory (Blau, 1974) in human interactions. Leaders gain status and influence over group members in return for demonstrating task competence and loyalty to the group. Hollander and Offermann (1990) call this type of explanation "a process-oriented transactional approach to leadership.... It emphasizes the implicit social exchange or transaction over time that exists between the leaders and followers, including reciprocal influence and interpersonal perception" (p. 181). Using this approach, Hollander (1958, 1986) had advanced the "idiosyncratic credit" model of leadership that explains why the innovative ideas of leaders gain acceptance among followers. According to this model, leaders earn such credits from followers' perceptions of their leaders' competence and loyalty. A leader can then use such credits that, in effect, represent the followers' trust, in order to influence followers' compliance and commitment to innovative goals.

Finally, leaders' influence on followers has also been explained by analyzing the motivational processes governing follower satisfaction and performance. A path-goal theory of leadership was first proposed by Evans (1970) and later advanced by House (1971) using the expectancy theory of motivation to account for leadership effectiveness. According to House and his associates (e.g., House & Dessler, 1974; House & Mitchell, 1974), each of the four types of leadership role behaviors, such as directive, achievement-oriented, supportive, and participative, influences followers by increasing the personal payoffs to them for group task accomplishments and "making the path to these payoffs easier to travel by clarifying it, reducing roadblocks and pitfalls, and increasing the opportunities for personal satisfaction en route" (House, 1971, p. 324). Similar motivational explanations for the effectiveness of various leadership activities have also been suggested by Oldham (1976), when he observes that leadership activities such as rewarding, setting goals, designing job and feedback systems, and so on heighten followers' motivation. Other researchers (e.g., Podsakoff, Todor, & Skov, 1982; Sims, 1977) have explained leadership effectiveness in terms of the behavior modification principles of contingent reinforcement. Maintaining influence over followers through the use of contingent reinforcement has also been interpreted as a form of transactional leadership (Avolio & Bass, 1988).

In summary, these modal trends have led to a focus on three major leadership role dimensions: (a) people concern, which manifests itself in a relationship orientation and consideration and supportive activities; (b) task concern, which focuses on achievement orientation and activities that emphasize initiating structure, goal setting, and facilitating task performance; and (c) concern for making and implementing decisions, which includes characteristics such as facilitating interaction and determination of the appropriateness of styles that range from autocratic and directive to consultative and participative. These specific role dimensions have been studied in situational contexts involving varied characteristics of three distinct elements: tasks, followers, and groups or organizations.

Most contingency theories of leadership consider these three elements as possible contingencies for understanding leadership effectiveness. Finally, the nature of the leader-follower influence process is also understood in terms of the three theoretical perspectives: control over valued resources, social exchange processes, and motivational dynamics. During the past quarter century, leadership contingency models dealing with the three behavior dimensions, the three situational elements and the three classes of explanations discussed above have dominated the scientific literature, both in the East (Misumi, 1988; Sinha, 1980) and the West (Fiedler, 1967; Heller, 1971; House, 1971; Vroom & Yetton, 1973).

▨ LIMITATIONS OF THE MODAL ORIENTATIONS

Recently, however, the leadership models discussed above have been considered to be too narrow and sterile (Hunt, 1984). The disappointment that has been expressed about these models relates to their failure to move beyond the simple social versus task dimensions, or autocratic versus participative dimensions, which underscored the work of early theorists (Bryman, 1986). However, the disappointment that is of greater significance is that they seem to ignore certain core aspects of leadership role behavior. These core aspects are the leader's formulation and articulation of a future vision or the formulation of goals for the followers, or the building of trust and credibility in the minds of followers, which is so crucial to develop in them a commitment to strive for the realization of the vision. If we just consider the last aspect—the building of trust and credibility in followers—we can see that it is much more enabling and enduring than is the case when followers' routine compliance is obtained to maintain the group's or the organization's status quo.

The narrowness of the existing theories and research on leadership is also reflected in the inadequate attention to the study of followers' behavior and their perceptions and motivations in following their leaders. As Hollander and Offermann (1990) point out, "Although the study of leadership has always presumed the existence of followers, their roles were viewed as essentially passive" (p. 182). Thus, there is a need for follower-centered approaches to leadership research. Such narrowness of the existing models stems from the research strategies employed to understand the phenomenon.

There are three main reasons for the existing models and the related research strategies. First, these models are based principally on small groups. When leadership is studied in small groups whether in a laboratory or in organizations, certain elements of leadership as observed in large corporations or in religious, social, and political organizations are missed. An example of a leadership element that could easily be missed when studies are based on small groups is the formulation of a mission or a strategic vision. Second, the studies of supervision in organizations have always used follower attitudes and behavior as dependent variables, rather than as antecedents or explanations for the leadership phenomenon. Consequently, these studies have neglected the follower-centered approaches, and to that extent the understanding of the leadership phenomenon from these studies is seriously distorted or incomplete.

Third, most leadership studies in organizational contexts have, in fact, been studies of supervision of day-to-day routine maintenance rather than the true phenomenon of leadership as observed in society. The core element of supervision or managership is the effective maintenance of the status quo, whereas a core element of leadership is to effectively bring about improvements, changes, and transformations in the existing system and in its members. In the organizational behavior literature, several scholars (Jago, 1982; Mintzberg, 1982a; Zaleznik, 1977) have acknowledged the distinction between leadership and managership. But this distinction has neither been taken seriously by researchers nor has it been sharply delineated for developing future research agendas. If it is to be taken seriously, a fundamental shift is imperative.

Instead of the current preoccupation with supervisory or managerial styles (task, people, participative orientations), the focus of leadership research should change to the study of other behavior dimensions such as visioning, articulating a vision, developing strategies to achieve the vision, and so on. These indeed are the crucial behaviors that are observed in leaders who bring about profound changes in their organizations and in their members (Bass, 1990b; Conger & Kanungo, 1988a). Likewise, the follower-centered approaches with an emphasis on follower perceptions and attributions in the leader-follower dynamics should be paid greater attention (Hollander & Offermann, 1990). This type of paradigm shift (Hunt, 1984) is already taking place, as can be seen by the recent emergence of interest in the charismatic and transformational leadership phenomenon (Bass, 1985; Burns, 1978; Conger, 1989; Conger & Kanungo, 1987; House, 1977) and follower attributions and the empowerment process (Conger & Kanungo, 1988c; Hollander & Offermann, 1990; Thomas & Velthouse, 1990).

▨ EMERGING FRONTIERS IN LEADERSHIP RESEARCH

To examine the new frontiers of leadership research, we will again draw on the three categories we have employed to explore past research efforts: (a) leader role behavior dimensions, (b) contingencies of leadership effectiveness, and (c) leadership influence processes.

Leader Role Behavior

Starting with the leader role dimension, there is a need to move beyond the task, social, and participative roles to those identified in the recent work on charismatic and transformational leadership (Bass, 1985; Bennis & Nanus, 1985; Conger, 1989; Conger & Kanungo, 1988b; House, 1977; House, Spangler, & Woycke, 1991; Shamir, House, & Arthur, 1989). More specifically, past research has underemphasized the complexity of two of the important dimensions of the leadership process as defined by Cartwright and Zander (1968): "setting group goals, moving the group toward its goals" (p. 304). The charismatic or transformational leadership research has directed particular attention to these areas in terms of role behavior. For example, recent explorations into the topic of strategic vision in the management literature have directed our attention to the leader's role in setting group goals at the organizational level. Although there is agreement on the significance of this role behavior (Bass, 1985; Bennis & Nanus, 1985; Conger & Kanungo, 1988a; House, 1977; Shamir et al., 1989; Sashkin, 1988; Westley & Mintzberg, 1988), the actual process of strategic visioning as a behavioral process is poorly understood.

As a result, two polar positions generally exist. One argues that the process is deliberate, rational, and therefore trainable (Sashkin, 1988). The other sees visioning by the leader as a more complex, emergent process (Conger, 1989; Westley & Mintzberg, 1988). These distinct positions raise several interesting research questions: (a) whether strategic visioning is indeed deliberate or emergent or both; (b) whether it might be possible for both deliberate and emergent visioning processes to occur simultaneously; and (c) whether under certain contextual conditions one process is more appropriate and feasible than the other. We know so little about this critical aspect of leader role behavior that it deserves more sustained and encompassing research attention.

The second area for exploration in terms of leader role behavior involves moving the group toward its goals. We know from the charismatic or transformational leadership literature that there is a consensus on the leader behavior characteristics that appear to be helpful. These characteristics are (a) emotional expressiveness, (b) articulation skills, (c) high activity level, and (d) exemplary modeling behavior (Conger & Kanungo, 1988d; House 1977). These behavioral attributes seem to facilitate trust, provide direction, and stimulate motivation in followers to achieve the vision for the group. There is also some limited agreement on whether leader behaviors such as unconventional behavior and risk-taking behavior affect followers' acceptance and attribution of leadership (Conger & Kanungo, 1988d). Generally, however, our knowledge of the exact nature of these leadership dynamics or how and when these leader behaviors influence followers' attitudes and behavior is poorly understood and requires further research attention. Nevertheless, the formulations of leadership in terms of the transformational leader role and the charismatic leader role provide an encouraging and positive first step in understanding the leadership phenomenon.

Bass (1985), who has been the principal proponent of the term *transformational leadership,* viewed it as being substantially different from transactional leadership. Thus, whereas transactional leaders ensure follower compliance through exchange of valued rewards, transformational leaders direct their efforts to bring followers to higher need levels and to outcomes that go well beyond the followers' self-interests. In other words, transformational leaders present to the followers the vision and its high ideals and values and encourage and help followers to incorporate these in their lives. The resulting internalization by the followers of the leader's ideals and values is the basis for the followers' enhanced commitment, efforts, and actions toward the realization of the vision. Although transformational leaders also engaged in transactional type behaviors, the characteristics of behaviors that were primarily responsible for the followers' internalization of the vision have been identified as charismatic—that is, engendering faith in and trust of the leader; consideration of or sensitivity to followers' needs; a statement of the vision in a manner that causes followers to reassess their priorities and activities (Bass, 1985).

Recently, Conger and Kanungo (1987, 1988b, 1992) developed a model that focuses on several behavioral dimensions of charismatic leadership within organizations. According to the model, followers attribute charisma to the leader based on their perceptions of the leader's behavior. Stated differently, the leader's observed behaviors are interpreted by followers as expressions of charisma. The Conger-Kanungo model proposes several distinguishing behavioral components in three distinct stages of the charismatic leadership process (see Figure 2.1). In Stage 1, the model distinguishes the perceived charismatic leadership role of managers from other leadership roles (task role, social role, or participative role) by the followers' perceptions of managers as reformers or agents of radical reform. In this role, followers perceive managers as individuals with a greater desire to change the status quo and a profoundly intense sensitivity to environmental opportunities and constraints as well as to followers' needs. Although these latter behaviors are necessary for all types of leader roles, they are particularly crucial for charismatic leadership because of the demands of the next stage of the process. For this reason, these behaviors should perhaps not be termed as distinguishing attributes, but as necessary and supporting features of the phenomenon.

The behaviors in Stage 2 consist of the formulation of an idealized future vision that is different from the status quo and yet shared by subordinates, and the ability to articulate this vision effectively in an inspirational manner. These behaviors clearly distinguish managers in charismatic leadership roles from the other roles. Finally, in Stage 3, managers are perceived to engage in exemplary acts that subordinates interpret as involving great personal risk and sacrifice. Through these behaviors, charismatic leaders are able to empower followers and engender trust, commitment, and loyalty. Charismatic leaders are seen to deploy innovative and unconventional means to achieve the vision.

An empirical study (Conger & Kanungo, 1994) of the Conger-Kanungo model confirmed six behavioral dimensions that relate to the three stages of the charismatic leadership process. Thus, "environmental sensitivity," "sensitivity to member needs," and "does not maintain status quo" relate to evalu-

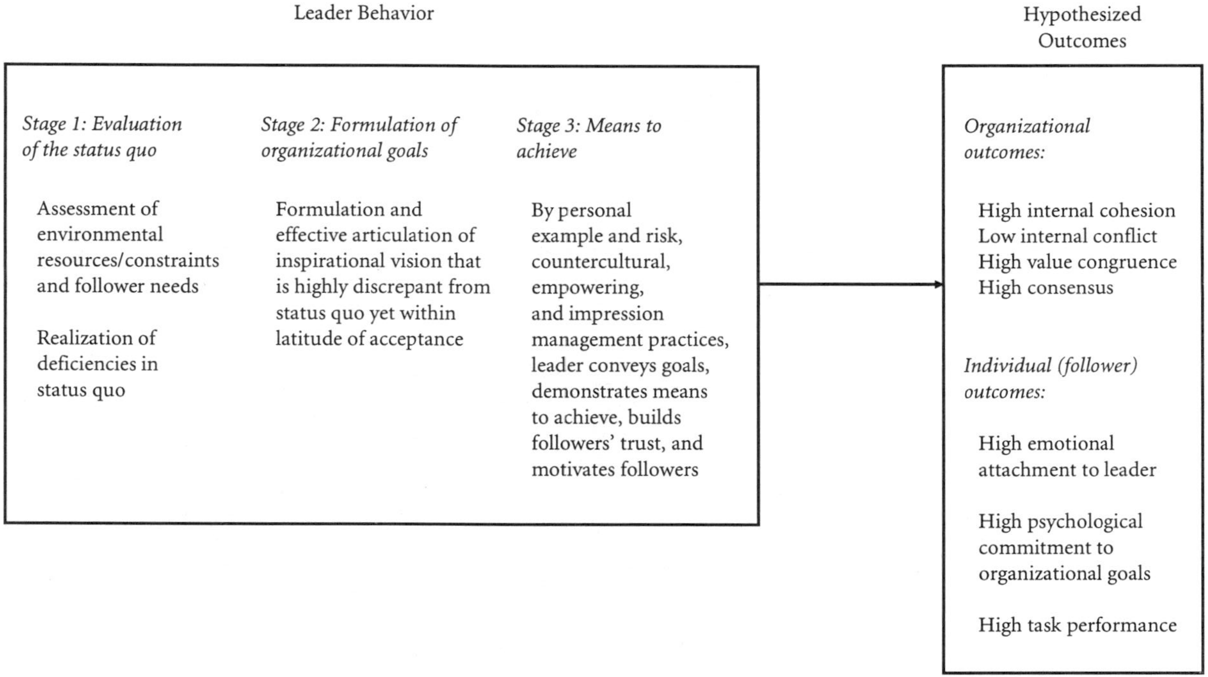

Leader Behavior

Stage 1: Evaluation of the status quo	Stage 2: Formulation of organizational goals	Stage 3: Means to achieve
Assessment of environmental resources/constraints and follower needs	Formulation and effective articulation of inspirational vision that is highly discrepant from status quo yet within latitude of acceptance	By personal example and risk, countercultural, empowering, and impression management practices, leader conveys goals, demonstrates means to achieve, builds followers' trust, and motivates followers
Realization of deficiencies in status quo		

Hypothesized Outcomes

Organizational outcomes:

High internal cohesion
Low internal conflict
High value congruence
High consensus

Individual (follower) outcomes:

High emotional attachment to leader

High psychological commitment to organizational goals

High task performance

Figure 2.1. The Conger-Kanungo Model of the Charismatic Leadership Process
SOURCE: Conger and Kanungo (1988b). Reprinted with permission.

25

ation of the status quo (Stage 1); "vision and articulation" relates to formula-tion of organizational goals (Stage 2); and "personal risk" and "unconventional behavior" relate to means to achieve (Stage 3). However, the behavioral dimen-sions of vision and articulation, unconventional behavior, personal risk and striving to change the status quo constitute the major features that distinguish the charismatic leadership role from the other leadership roles.

When we compare the formulation of the transformational leader role (Bass, 1985) and that of the charismatic leader role (Conger & Kanungo, 1994), we find some overlap, especially on the vision and the follower sensitivity dimensions. However, the major distinction between the transformational and the charismatic formulations relates not so much to the leader's behavior but to the perspective from which the leadership phenomenon is viewed. The charismatic theories and research view leadership from the perspective of the *perceived leader behavior;* the transformational theories, so far, focus mainly on *followers' outcomes.* One can trace these theoretical perspectives to the contexts in which they were developed. Thus, the original conceptualization of trans-formational leadership by Burns (1978) was developed in the context of politics and focused on leadership effectiveness and experience as a function of fol-lower needs satisfaction. On the other hand, the earlier formulation of char-ismatic leadership had its roots in sociology (Weber, 1925/1968) and was primarily concerned with leadership effectiveness as a function of leader be-havior and the context in which leaders find themselves. In essence, then, the two formulations—charismatic and transformational—in the organizational literature are highly complementary (Conger & Kanungo, 1994).

Contingencies of Leadership Effectiveness

Within the context of charismatic or transformational leadership roles, one can also examine the contingencies of leadership effectiveness when effec-tiveness is measured in terms of transformational—as opposed to transac-tional—influence on followers. At least three categories of contingencies need to be explored in future research: the task context, the follower characteristics, and the social-cultural environment within which the leader operates. The task context within which a leader sets group goals or formulates a vision as a future target for the group to achieve can act as an important contingency for leadership effectiveness. There may be certain contextual conditions that are more ideal, or at least more helpful, in facilitating the charismatic or transformational leadership process. For instance, a context in crisis or one with important shortcomings may heighten the leader's attractiveness and influence. Some scholars also believe that the leader may play an active, if not primary, role in creating a belief among followers that a contextual crisis exists in order to achieve leadership effectiveness.

For example, Conger and Kanungo (1988a) argue that charismatic leaders, because of their intolerance of the status quo, tend to quickly identify and exaggerate existing deficiencies in the environment and articulate these to subordinates. Such leaders are sensitive to shortcomings and are able to discern how environmental constraints frustrate followers' needs. Thus, the identification of crisis in the task context is partly due to the deficiencies in the status quo and partly determined by the way in which charismatic leaders relate to their contexts. In other words, a crisis situation is taken advantage of by the leader, and to some extent, the situation is the making of the leader's actions and behavior. Explorations into the dynamics of how task contexts act as a contingency are needed in the future. Both theoretical development and empirical verification of how, why, and when leaders identify and articulate crises and deficiencies in their environment need to be on the agenda for future research.

Besides "crisis" in the task context, leadership effectiveness can also be influenced by the leader's perception of unexplored positive opportunities in the larger environment. As mentioned, a leader's transformational influence may be enhanced when the leader identifies or articulates a crisis in the status quo, but at the same time he or she may also identify a potential opportunity within the environment and articulate an inspiring future vision that fully taps that opportunity. Depending on the emphasis the leader places while relating to the context (either on the status quo or on the vision), his or her influence could be characterized as a crisis or ideological influence. Future research attention should be directed toward exploring the extent to which crisis and opportunities in the context are used by leaders to foster their influence.

From the viewpoint of follower characteristics as possible contingencies, there are two important issues that require significant attention—first, the process of leadership attribution by followers, and second, the dispositional characteristics of followers themselves. Starting with the first issue, it is obvious that to be effective as a leader one must first be recognized as such. This recognition or attribution of leadership status is an important measure of leadership effectiveness. When we consider its importance in understanding the leadership process, it is indeed ironic that we understand so little about it. As Calder (1977) argues, leadership is a label that followers attribute to leaders performing certain behaviors. The followers' "belief that a certain leadership quality produces a certain behavior [that] is transformed into the expectation that an instance of the behavior implies the existence of the quality" (p. 198). Calder (1977) and Meindl et al. (1985) have stimulated our thinking in terms of the mechanics of this leadership attribution process itself.

The implications for future research are that we need to examine the factors that followers consider when attributing outcomes to leadership and specifically to a particular form of leadership such as the charismatic or transformational forms. Bryman (1986) points out, however, that experimental and quantitative approaches to explore this issue may be premature. Instead, more subtle, qualitative approaches at this stage may more fully capture the range of criteria that followers take into account when accepting and attributing leadership status to the leader. Our understanding of the circumstances and the processes by which leadership is invoked as an explanation in followers' minds is very limited.

The second issue of follower characteristics that needs further exploration concerns the possibility that certain dispositional attributes may enhance the receptivity and commitment of followers to a leader and as such leadership effectiveness. For example, various researchers in the charismatic/transformational literature have suggested that certain follower predispositions may in part be responsible for behavioral outcomes such as a high level of emotional commitment to the leader, heightened motivation, willing obedience to the leader, greater group cohesion, and a sense of empowerment (Conger & Kanungo, 1988d). They hypothesize that charismatic leaders have followers who tend to be submissive and dependent (Downton, 1973). Low self-esteem and strong feelings of uncertainty are further thought to characterize these individuals and in turn foster a receptiveness to the self-confident and directive charismatic leader (Galanter, 1982; Lodahl, 1982). Directly related to the issue of dispositions are the psychological and behavioral outcomes of charismatic leadership on followers. We know from research by House, Woycke, and Fodor (1988) that charismatic leadership can induce in followers trust and obedience to the leader, and a willingness to accept and to be enthusiastically committed to the leader's mission. Some of these may have negative outcomes, as evidenced by Conger's (1990) recent discussion of the liabilities of followership. Both of these issues require further empirical exploration.

Consideration of the followers' perceptions of the context as possible contingencies of charismatic/transformational leadership effectiveness suggests that when followers experience psychological distress, transformational influence is facilitated. In other words, when the context evokes feelings of high uncertainty (Conger, 1985), helplessness, powerlessness, and alienation (Kanungo, 1982) among followers, conditions become ripe for a leader's influence within organizations. Followers become "charisma hungry" when they experience a loss of control over their environment, when their needs and expectations are frustrated because of perceived environmental barriers and threats, when they see an uncertain future, or when they experience an identity crisis because of a state of anomie (decline of old values and rituals). Lee Iacocca's charismatic influence on Chrysler's employees can be partly explained by the way that Chrysler employees perceived their context. They perceived significant future uncertainty (fear of company bankruptcy and the loss of jobs), which caused them to suffer psychological distress and consequently made them more susceptible to Iacocca's influence.

Both Bass (1988) and Kets de Vries (1988) talk of perceived anomie, upheaval, and crisis in the environment leading to a sense of helplessness and regressive forms of follower behavior, such as unquestioning and blind trust in the leader. However, the psychological processes underlying helplessness (Garber & Seligman, 1980) and alienation (Kanungo, 1982) and the identification of specific organizational conditions (Martinko & Gardner, 1982) that promote such psychological states among followers have received little attention. Future studies should explore this issue in greater depth.

Finally, in the leadership effectiveness literature, there has been, with few exceptions (such as Sinha, 1990), little emphasis on culture as a contingency variable. We suspect that there are innumerable cultural dynamics that influence the leadership process (Kanungo & Conger, 1989). For example, followers are more likely to attribute leadership to an individual when they perceive his or her leadership behavior to be culturally appropriate and in congruence with their own cultural values. Thus, in a traditional organizational or national culture that subscribes to conservative modes of behavior among its members and the use of conventional means to achieve organizational objectives, leaders who engage in excessive unconventional behavior may be viewed more as deviants than as charismatic or transformational leaders. Also, individuals in leadership positions whose visions fail to incorporate important values and lack relevance for the organizational culture are unlikely to be attributed leadership status.

Certain behavioral components of the charismatic leadership role, as mentioned earlier, may be more critical and effective sources for attributions of leadership in some organizational or cultural contexts than in others. The relative importance and specific characteristics of a particular behavior category will most likely differ from one cultural context to the next. For example, different cultures will have different modes of articulation, vision formulation, impression management, and so on. Explorations of these variations are critical for identifying leadership effectiveness in different cultures.

Leadership Influence Processes

Turning to the third issue of leadership influence mechanisms, we find that transactional or social exchange approaches to leadership have been extensively explored (Hollander, 1964, 1978; Hollander & Offermann, 1990). What deserves our attention at this point are the mechanisms of the transformational effects of leadership on followers. We have a very limited understanding of these influence dynamics.

Explanations for why and how leaders exert transformational influence on followers who in turn develop and maintain their emotional involvement with a leader principally come from two sources: social psychological theories of influence processes (French & Raven, 1959; Kelman, 1958) and Freudian theories of ego defense mechanisms (Freud, 1946). For example, Conger and Kanungo (1988a) have proposed that the charismatic leader-follower relationship is one of expert and referent power (French & Raven, 1959) where followers accept the leader's influence primarily because they perceive the leader's expertise and develop a liking for and identity with the leader. Howell (1988) explains the relationship in terms of both identification and internalization using Kelman's (1958) theory of social influence.

Shamir et al. (1989) postulate that transformational leaders influence through implicating the self-concept of follower. They increase the intrinsic value of efforts and goals by linking them to important aspects of followers' self-concepts. From the Freudian perspective, a psychological process involving unconscious tendencies has been elaborated by Kets de Vries (1988). Followers try to resolve the conflict between who they are and what they wish to become by projecting their ego ideals onto the leader, and thereby make the leader their own conscience. The leader thus gains influence by being a model of what followers consciously or unconsciously wish for themselves (Downton,

1973). These explanations, however, remain at a speculative level and require empirical validation in future research.

Another area of significant debate centers on the leader's power orientation and its impact on influence tactics. House (1977) has proposed that charismatic leaders possess a high need for power, which in turn motivates them to assume the leader role. Drawing on McClelland's (1975) work on socialized and personalized power, some researchers argue that charismatic/ transformational leaders who are high in self-serving activity inhibition become "socialized leaders" expressing their need for power through socially constructive behavior and that it is only through this behavior that the transformational influence process is able to take effect. Other leaders, low in self-serving activity inhibition, become "personalized leaders" who express and satisfy their need for power through personally dominant and authoritarian behavior negating the transformational influence process (Howell, 1988). We feel that this conceptualization of charismatic leadership in terms of power orientation requires significant exploration, particularly with reference to the effectiveness of the transformational and transactional influence processes.

A second area of the influence dimension that requires further exploration concerns the process of empowerment. In our earlier discussion of the modal orientations, three mechanisms for explaining leadership influence were identified. All three mechanisms explain the transactional nature of leadership influence processes. There is a need to go beyond these to explain the charismatic/transformational influence process. Empowerment is one important area for explaining such influence. Traditionally, empowerment has been viewed more as a transactional process of sharing power and resources. However, several researchers (Conger & Kanungo, 1988c; Thomas & Velthouse, 1990) have argued that the empowerment process should be viewed as a process of enabling followers through the enhancement of their personal self-efficacy beliefs and intrinsic task motivation. Viewed in this way, leadership influence is a process of transforming followers' self-concepts and attitudes toward the task and goal set for the group. Thomas and Velthouse's (1990) model of empowerment defined around increased intrinsic task motivation suggests that critical to the process of empowerment is an understanding of the workers' interpretive styles and global beliefs. Empirical research needs to be conducted to verify their hypotheses. Likewise, the nature and mechanisms underlying the empowerment process as suggested by the self-efficacy model proposed by Conger and Kanungo (1988c) need to be empirically validated.

N CONCLUSION

In conclusion, the general field of leadership research needs to be explored along both content and process dimensions. In the area of content dimensions, there is a need for a shift in focus from supervisory/managerial behavior (e.g., consideration, task, participation) to leadership behavior (e.g., visioning, goal-setting, empowering). Also, there needs to be an additional shift in research focus from followers' need satisfaction to attributional, dispositional, and perceptual dynamics. Third, research attention needs to be redirected from the exclusive preoccupation with specific task characteristics in small groups to the study of the larger context within which tasks are accomplished. This should also include a study of cultural variables as possible contingencies. Along process dimensions, past research has emphasized largely the transactional influence processes. Future research must be directed toward exploring the basis of transformational influence.

Although a significant challenge awaits leadership research, it is necessary to recognize that effective leadership depends not only on what behaviors the leader performs and how proficiently these are performed but also on the ethics and morality of these behaviors. For this purpose, the chapters that follow examine, in light of ethical and moral considerations, the motives underlying the leader's behavior (Chapter 3) and the processes the leader uses to influence the followers' behavior (Chapter 4).

Ethical Dimensions
in Leadership Motivation

The several examples cited in the first chapter clearly demonstrate that when leaders compromise their ethical standards they do harm, often irreparable, in terms of the immediate physical and moral suffering to others within and outside the organization. They also create an atmosphere of ethical cynicism that is not conducive to forming a sound sense and understanding of the need for ethics and ethical behavior. It is not uncommon for many in business to regard "business ethics" as an oxymoron. Effective organizational leaders need ethics as fish need water and human beings need air.

What specifically do we understand and mean by *ethics?* The *Concise Oxford English Dictionary* (1964) defines ethics as "relating to morals . . . treating of moral questions . . . rules of conduct . . . the whole field of moral science" (p. 415). When we explore further the meaning of *moral,* we find it defined as "concerned with character or disposition, or with the distinction between right and wrong" (p. 784). Clearly, ethics and morality are interchangeable terms. Thus, what is ethical is moral, and what is unethical is immoral. Morals or ethics go well beyond etiquette, protocol, and even the mere observance of the laws of the country. It is not a question of an act being legal or illegal but whether the act is good or evil. A legal act may not necessarily be a morally good act. For example, at the Nuremberg trials all the accused had committed acts that were legal but not morally good.

According to Thomas Aquinas, a morally good act has three parts or factors: (a) the objective act itself, (b) the subjective motive of the actor, and

(c) the situation or circumstances in which the act is done. Thus, to act justly is an objectively good act, just as to murder is an objectively evil act. The actor must always have good intentions. For example, making charitable donations only to avoid paying income tax vitiates the moral goodness of an objectively good act. The situation or circumstances must also be considered. Thus, giving alms to the poor is, other things being equal, a morally good act, but refusing alms to the poor person who you know would spend it on his or her alcoholic addiction is equally a morally good act. Hence, if an act is to be morally good it must be right in respect to all the three parts. The controversies in normative theories of ethics exist because these theories or ethical systems emphasize one part to the neglect of the other parts.

In assessing the morality of an act, one cannot focus only on the objective moral law and ignore the individual's motive and the relative circumstances. If we do, then the act of killing, even though that was the only way of defending oneself, would be an immoral act. Theories or theorists that take such a position might be said to engage in "unthinking legalism." The ethical system of moral subjectivism concentrates on only the second factor—that is, the subjective motive. Thus, a moral subjectivist defends his actions entirely in terms of his or her own motive and pays no attention to the nature or characteristics of the objective act and the circumstances of the situation. An example of moral subjectivism would be the views expressed in a recent newsletter of a Mensa chapter in Los Angeles, which states that people whose mental defects make them incapable of living in society should be humanely dispatched as soon as they are identified ("Mensa Chapter," 1995, p. A6).

The third popular ethical system today is "situation ethics." This system focuses only on the situation, or the situation and the motive—as is the case when one argues that the end justifies the means. The recent public discussion of the morality of the atomic bombing of Hiroshima and Nagasaki to end World War II underscores this point. Even the "just war" theory does not provide a justification for an indiscriminate use of means to achieve an end. The intended and unintended consequences of the means that are used ought to be examined—that is, the objective nature of the acts that are involved. If we do not, then we deny that we should also consider the first factor that makes an act moral—the objective nature of the act (Kreeft, 1990).

It is beyond the scope of this book to discuss the differences among moral philosophers and their ethical systems. This has been dealt with quite adequately in the several books on ethics and moral issues in business (e.g., Barry, 1978). We would, however, make two points. First, it is important to recognize that despite the differences in the normative theories of ethics, there is a substantial agreement among people that "some types of actions are better than others, and better in an unconditional way, not just better for a particular person or better in relation to a particular set of cultural norms" (Spaemann, 1989, p. 12). For example, when it became known that Maximilian Kolbe, the Polish priest, gave up his life in the Auschwitz concentration camp in order to save a man who had a wife and children, this act was regarded throughout the world as a heroic act of the highest moral standard. This is because morally good acts are based on moral laws that are universal because they incorporate fundamental values such as truth, goodness, beauty, courage, and justice. These values are found in all cultures, although cultures may differ with regard to the application of these values.

> For instance, in some societies, suicide is thought to be courageous, in others it is thought to be cowardly. But no society prefers cowardice to courage. Some societies let a man have four wives, others only one, but no society says a man may simply take any woman he wants. (Kreeft, 1990, p. 34)

Second, one such area of agreement relates to altruism as a principle of moral behavior. Altruism is highly regarded in all cultures as the epitome of sound moral principles. Even those whose behavior is inconsistent with this moral principle rarely deny its validity. On the contrary, they might argue that circumstances or conditions prevent them from acting altruistically. Our thesis is that organizational leaders are truly effective only when they are motivated by a concern for others, when their actions are invariably guided primarily by the criteria of "the benefit to others even if it results in some cost to self." The underlying rationale or purpose for having a leader in a group or an organization is to move it toward the pursuit of objectives that, when attained, would produce benefits to both the organization and its members. The leader's efforts and strategies in the areas of planning, controlling, and coordinating are justified and assume meaning and significance only to the extent that these are intended to serve the interests of the organization and its members. Because the "other"—that is, the organization and its members—is the raison d'être of the leader's efforts, the altruistic motive becomes the only consistent motive for the leader role.

Therefore, leadership effectiveness is ensured only by altruistic acts that reflect the leader's incessant desire and concern to benefit others despite the risk of personal cost inherent in such acts. For this reason, the sections that follow will address the following questions: What are the nature and characteristics of altruism? What are its manifest behaviors? Why is it essential for leaders to be altruistic?

◪ ALTRUISM: ITS CHARACTERISTICS AND MANIFEST BEHAVIORS

A certain man went down from Jerusalem to Jericho, and fell among thieves, which stripped him of his raiment, and wounded him, and departed, leaving him half dead. And by chance there came down a certain priest that way, and when he saw him, he passed by on the other side. And likewise a Levite, when he was at the place, came and looked on him, and passed by on the other side. But a certain Samaritan, as he journeyed, came where he was, and when he saw him, he had compassion on him. And went to him, and bound up his wounds, pouring in oil and wine, and set him on his own beast, and brought him to an inn, and took care of him. And on the morrow when he departed, he took out two pence, and gave them to the host, and said unto him, "Take care of him, and whatsoever thou spendest more, when I come again, I will repay thee." (Luke 10:30-35)

This biblical story captures the essence of altruistic behavior. We see in this story three types of behaviors. First, the behavior of the thieves, who deliberately harmed the traveler for their personal gain. Second, the priest and the Levite, who demonstrated complete apathy to avoid the personal costs or inconvenience from being involved. Third, the Samaritan, who went through considerable self-sacrifice to help the traveler. Clearly, the Samaritan's behavior is commonly seen as altruistic, whereas the other two types of behaviors are perceived as egotistic. The Samaritan is seen as being motivated by a concern for the benefit of others and a disregard for his own personal costs. On the other hand, the behavior of the thieves, the priest, and the Levite is perceived as motivated by a concern for benefits and costs to themselves and by a disregard for the benefits and costs to others. Of course, as will be discussed later, a clear moral difference exists between the behavior of the thieves and that of the priest and Levite. But these are grouped together because their behavior can be categorized as "benefiting self." It is the criteria of "benefiting others" versus benefiting self that distinguishes altruistic from egotistic behaviors.

What Is Altruism?

Social psychologists define altruism in two ways. First, it is defined as an attributed dispositional intent to help others, a "willingness to sacrifice one's welfare for the sake of another" (Krebs, 1982, p. 55), as behavior intended to benefit others without the expectation of an external reward (Macaulay & Berkowitz, 1970). Second, it is defined in terms of the manifest behavior and its consequences without any reference to one's dispositional intentions. Thus, altruism is that behavior "that renders help to another person" (Worchel, Cooper, & Goethals, 1988, p. 394) regardless of the intention of the help provider. The first type of definition can be said to refer to altruism as an internal state; the second type refers to it as a behavior with consequences. Because it is often difficult to identify the help provider's dispositional intentions, researchers have preferred to define altruism as a form of overt behavior that benefits others. As a behavioral construct, altruism has a much broader scope, which covers both intentions and actions. The actions take many forms of prosocial behavior such as charity, helping, cooperation, and empowering, which benefit others regardless of whether these are intended to be selfless or otherwise. As a behavioral construct, one can also explore the underlying motivational processes that energize, direct, and maintain altruistic intentions and behaviors in individuals. These elements of altruism are elaborated further in the following sections.

What Are the Reasons for Altruistic Behavior?

The existing motivational theories confirm and support our intuitive understanding that all human acts seek to achieve some purpose or goal. Altruistic acts also share this basic characteristic of human acts. Although altruistic acts are directed primarily for the express purpose of benefiting others, these acts also satisfy some needs of the individual. This latter characteristic has given rise to the "hedonistic paradox," which questions the existence of altruism. The question is posed thus: Suppose an act that is intended to benefit others does, in fact, benefit the other person as well as the actor. How, then, can it be termed altruistic? In dealing with this question, we need to recognize a common assumption held by psychologists that all behavior, whether directed toward benefiting one's own self or another, is energized by some needs or inner drives without which human behavior would simply not occur. It is, therefore, to be expected that altruistic behaviors must necessarily stem from an inner need state. These behaviors are directed primarily to fulfill the individual's objective or intention of benefiting others. In the process of meeting this objective, the behaviors do satisfy some needs of the individual, but the existence in human beings of the deeper-level need for altruism that is the source of these behaviors cannot be denied. For this reason, the hedonistic paradox that questions the existence of altruism is much like the chicken-and-egg conundrum, a nonissue.

Altruistic behavior defined as benefiting others can stem from internal need states such as a "nurturance" need postulated by Murray (1938) and later by Jackson (1967). Psychologists generally view nurturance as a learned psychological need, and sociobiologists argue that genetic preprogramming underlies the altruistic behavior mechanism (Wilson, 1978). It is rather difficult to determine the validity of a genetic basis for altruism. For this reason, we shall examine the two major explanations offered by social psychologists that help us understand how human beings acquire the need for nurturance or altruism. The two explanations are anchored in the notions of the reciprocity norm and the social responsibility norm. Through the socialization process, we develop these internal norms that operate as a motivational force and guide our behavior. When we refer to the socialization process, we include the individual's religious formation and related spiritual transformation, which serve as a powerful reinforcement of altruistic behavior.

Human beings develop an internal moral code of reciprocity that dictates that individuals will help those who have helped them (Gouldner, 1960). This norm generally applies when people are interacting with their equals or with those who possess greater resources. However, when individuals deal with their dependents who are unable to reciprocate, then the inner moral code of social responsibility may be evoked. The norm of social responsibility refers to an internalized belief that to help others without any consideration in return, such as an expected future personal benefit, is a moral imperative (Berkowitz, 1972; Schwartz, 1975). Such internalized beliefs regarding social and moral obligations constitute the basis of an altruistic motive that, in turn, energizes altruistic behavior.

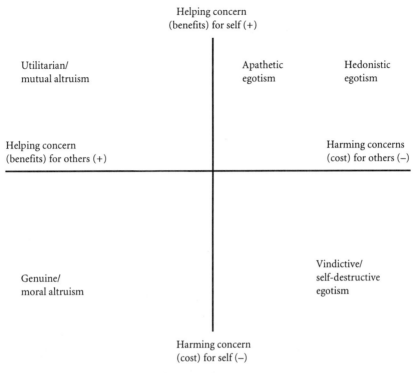

Figure 3.1. Forms of Altruistic and Egotistic Behavior

The Manifest Behaviors of Altruism

The different forms of altruistic behavior can be identified and distinguished from the different forms of egotistic behavior in terms of the polar dimensions presented in Figure 3.1 (Kanungo & Conger, 1993).

The two dimensions are behavior reflecting (in its consequences) a concern for benefiting or harming others and behavior reflecting (in its consequences) a concern for benefiting or harming oneself. The two axes in Figure 3.1 represent these two dimensions, which prove useful to analyze the behaviors in the biblical story. For example, when a behavior reflects a helping concern (or deriving benefits) for self but a harming concern for others, it represents what we call *hedonistic egotism*—as is the case with the behavior of the thieves. Often a behavior reflects helping concern for oneself with no apparent concern for others—either actively providing help or causing harm to others. Such behavior can be termed *apathetic egotism* and describes the behavior of the priest and the Levite.

Egotistic behavior can also take the form of *vindictive* or *self-destructive egotism*. It reflects a harming concern for both others and one's own self. This behavior is not found in our biblical story, but in personal and organizational contexts, an individual who exhibits such behavior generally adopts an "I will take you down with me" attitude. The violent manifestations of such behavior in the workplace, for example, disgruntled and dissatisfied employees gunning down their managers, is often reported in the media. It is, however, not uncommon to come across relatively milder forms of such behavior in the workplace, for example, managers, motivated by vendetta, suppressing critical information or being unwilling to surrender resources even when they recognize that these actions would adversely affect their own units as well as the organization.

In contrast to these forms of egotistic behavior, altruistic behavior always reflects a helping concern for others. When such a concern is combined with a concern for one's own self-interest, the behavior can be called *utilitarian* or *mutual altruism*. The innkeeper in the biblical story demonstrated utilitarian altruism because he helped the injured traveler after being assured of compensation by the Samaritan. The motivational basis of utilitarian altruism is the expectation about the mutually beneficial consequences of the obligatory behavior. The last behavior category depicted in Figure 3.1 reflects a helping concern for others without any regard for self-interest, even when such concern involves considerable personal sacrifice or inconvenience—that is, harming self-interest. This behavior can be categorized as *genuine* or *moral altruism,* as demonstrated by the behavior of the Samaritan. The primary motivational force behind moral altruism is the internalized social responsibility norm or moral imperative. Moral philosophers may argue about different normative theories of ethics or morality. However, people in every part of the globe, in every culture, in every age—ancient, medieval, modern, or contemporary— will be unanimous in conceding that this Samaritan truly deserves the title of the good Samaritan.

The values inherent in the choice of "others before myself" or moral altruism are universal and form part of the heritage of all cultures. To illustrate this point, we cite examples from two religious traditions and cultures—the west European and the Hindu. Both have fundamentally different approaches to the sources of religious truth that illumine the path to moral behavior. The west European religious traditions have been formed by the thinking of both the Greeks and the Romans and by Judaism and Christianity. Hinduism—or, more appropriately, the Hindu view of life—is based on religious truths that have been expounded by the *rishiis* (the sages) and are contained essentially in the tales of two epics, the Ramayana and the Mahabharata. Despite these differences, we find interesting parallels in the hierarchy of values in relation to the "self-or-other" question. In both religious cultures, the self-or-other relationship can be considered at broadly three levels. The lowest level focuses on behaviors exclusively geared to the gratification of the self, for example, *eros* in Western traditions or *kama* in Hindu traditions. The next level corresponds to behaviors primarily motivated by familial considerations, helping those who are already close to you: *philia* in Western traditions or *prema* in Hindu traditions. The highest level consists of behaviors performed for the benefit of others, even if it comes at the cost of one's self: *agape* in Western traditions or *mokshya* in Hindu traditions.

◪ WHY IS IT ESSENTIAL FOR LEADERS TO BE ALTRUISTIC?

In our discussion on the modal orientations of leadership in Chapter 2, we identified the effective organizational leader role as one that fundamentally involves moving the organization from the status quo to a future desired goal. For this purpose, the charismatic leader performs a set of behaviors in three stages. As described previously, in the first stage, the leader assesses the environment with a view to identifying the deficiencies in the status quo and the potential opportunities consistent with the organization's resources and constraints, and the abilities, needs, and aspirations of organizational members. This environmental assessment leads, in the second stage, to the formulation and articulation of an idealized vision, which is discrepant from the status quo but nevertheless one that embodies a perspective shared by organizational members. Finally, in the third stage, the leader initiates steps to achieve the vision. The basic nature and thrust of these steps are strategies and interventions that are designed to empower the followers. Thus, the leader behaviors—particularly in the last stage—enable the followers to clearly perceive that the leader is trustworthy and has the expertise and capacity to persevere in the effort needed to realize the vision.

The leader behaviors in the three stages should provide direction, engender trust, and stimulate motivation in the followers to engage in activities that would achieve the vision. Now, if we analyze the leader's behaviors in the three stages in terms of the altruistic-egotistic dimensions, we can readily conclude that these behavioral attributes can only be demonstrated by a leader who is motivated by a high degree of moral altruism. Thus, the typical behaviors in the first stage—the environmental assessment stage—are characterized by a heightened sensitivity to environmental opportunities and constraints, and to the needs of the followers. A leader whose gaze and focus is turned inward to the self, and the self's concerns and interests become the all-consuming passion and obsession, is prevented from being open and sensitive to others. Such a leader might be dissatisfied with the status quo and present proposals to change it. But these proposals, even though they constitute a radical reform of the status quo, will not be well received by the followers to the degree that the leader's self-orientation would not consider the followers' needs and aspirations. In contrast, a concern for the welfare of the organization and its members is the primary preoccupation that underlies the behaviors demanded of the charismatic leadership role from the very beginning of the charismatic leadership process. For this reason, managers in a charismatic leadership role are more likely to be perceived by followers both as stern critics of the status quo and as benevolent reformers or agents of radical change.

In the second stage—the vision formulation and articulation stage—the critical behaviors of the charismatic leadership role are the formulation of a shared but idealized future vision and the effective articulation of this vision in an inspirational manner. The focus of both sets of behaviors is on others— the followers. The vision is undoubtedly the product of the leader's efforts in the environmental assessment stage. One might say that it is the expression of the person's beliefs and values, ideas and ideals, and unusual or creative discernment or perception of the opportunities that the organization can seize. Viewed in this way, the formulation of the vision appears to be very much the fruit of an individual's efforts. However, the realization of the idealized vision depends to a large extent on the followers' perception that it is a shared vision.

It is important to explore the notions of a shared, idealized vision. As alluded to previously, a shared vision is one that embodies the perspective of the followers and, in effect, meets their needs and aspirations. The idealized characteristic can be said to take the vision a big step further. It creates in followers an awakening, a realization that the vision expresses their most profound yearnings for a state that, until now, they could not meaningfully articulate and much less believe to be ever possible. When leaders advocate an idealized vision or future goal for the organization, and influence followers to move toward it, they assume considerable personal risks. Their willingness to take these risks is largely prompted by a sense of altruistic mission. On the other hand, those who work to maintain the status quo when the interests and needs of the organization and its members demand change often do so to avoid the personal risks of change and to cling to the benefits, power, and influence that the status quo confers on them. In this case, we see that the desire to preserve one's self-interest clearly overrides the concern for the interests of others.

Furthermore, the charismatic leader's effectiveness in this stage depends equally on the articulation of the vision. Because, as just discussed, the vision touches the very core of the followers' thoughts, feelings, and aspirations, the leader should communicate it in a manner that followers perceive to be genuinely natural, without any affectation or the use of gimmicks in its presentation. Clearly, a leader who is not motivated by a passionate and sincere care and concern, as well as a deep and abiding respect for others, will experience great difficulty in formulating and articulating the vision with the desired characteristics. Although effective organizational leaders engage in inspirational articulation of the idealized vision that reflects their altruistic motives, they also express them in several other ways. They express their strong beliefs in their own capability and in the capabilities of their followers to realize the vision. Through the expression of such beliefs, the leaders demonstrate their trust and confidence in their followers. It also provides followers with opportunities to assess the leader's selfless commitment to the vision. When followers perceive that the leader does not trust them and does not show confidence in their capabilities, that the leader is more concerned with protecting his or her own self-interest, then the articulation, however inspirational it might sound, will not cause the leader to be effective.

The focus on others is much more evident in the third stage—the implementation stage. The underlying intent of the behaviors in this stage is to motivate followers to achieve the vision by empowering them and developing their trust in the leader and the vision. For this purpose, the leader engages in modeling or exemplary acts, innovative and unconventional, that often involve great personal risks and sacrifices (Conger & Kanungo, 1988c). The inconvenience and pain and even the losses experienced by the leader in this process have to be perceived by the followers as more than an exercise in the satisfaction of the leader's masochistic desires. Rather, the followers must perceive these acts to be rooted in the leader's sincere desire to move followers toward the attainment of the shared vision. The leader also provides verbal encouragement and assistance in solving problems so that the followers may develop the necessary task-related self-efficiency, self-confidence, and self-reliance. To ensure and encourage the personal growth and development of the followers, effective leaders adopt empowerment strategies to influence followers, whereas ineffective leaders have to resort to control strategies. The nature and effects of these influence processes and their ethical implications will be discussed in the next chapter.

▧ HOW DOES ALTRUISM RELATE TO THE AFFILIATION, POWER, AND ACHIEVEMENT MOTIVES?

The preceding brief discussion of the leader's motivation in the three stages of the charismatic leadership process suggests that the behavioral attributes that are absolute imperatives for effective leadership can only be demonstrated by a leader who is motivated by a high degree of moral altruism. In other words, the satisfaction of the individual's altruistic need is the paramount condition for effective leadership. However, the existing leadership literature seems to ignore the altruistic need and instead suggests that effective leadership is motivated by a set of other needs such as the need for affiliation, the need for power, and the need for achievement (McClelland & Burnham, 1995). These needs have played a critical role in leader motivation in the different modal orientations of leadership discussed in the previous chapter. For example, the social-oriented leadership role is motivated by a need for affiliation; the task-oriented leadership role is motivated by needs for power and achievement; the autocratic-participative leadership role is motivated by needs for power, achievement, and affiliation. Such a limited focus on the motivational dynamics of leadership has had two undesirable consequences. First, it ignored the more profound motive of altruism, which is *the* critical ingredient of effective leadership. The second consequence follows from the first: By ignoring the altruistic motive, the discussion and study of the leadership phenomenon essentially avoided the moral and ethical issues that are involved in leadership.

We do recognize that it is appropriate and proper to study leadership behavior as being caused by a set of needs, such as the needs for power, achievement, and affiliation. In fact, without studying the overt behaviors generated by these needs it might not be possible to obtain, at least, an initial understanding of the basis of effective leadership. However, it is necessary to probe further whether these needs do, by themselves, provide a reasonably comprehensive understanding of the motivational dynamics of leadership. Our thesis is that these needs explain the basis of effective leadership only to the extent that they are a manifestation of the overarching altruistic need. Stated differently, the affiliative, power, and achievement needs might be viewed as the *operative* needs that provide a starting point to understanding leadership role effectiveness, whereas it is the presence of the deeper, *underlying* altruistic motive that better explains leader effectiveness. It is our intention to show that leader behaviors are ineffective when guided solely by one or more of these needs with a total disregard for altruism. On the other hand, leader behaviors are effective when motivated by these needs as an operative manifestation or expression of altruism.

The need for affiliation is dominant in the motivation of the social-oriented leader. Leaders who are high on affiliation motivation regard warm and friendly relationships with their followers as extremely important and, therefore, make considerable effort to be sensitive to followers' feelings and to conform to their wishes. These characteristics of the need for affiliation would suggest a concern for others and, hence, are compatible with the characteristics of the altruistic motive. However, Boyatzis (1973) posited two manifestations of the need for affiliation. One is "avoidance" affiliation; the other is "approach" affiliation. Avoidance affiliation is "a concern with the maintenance of relationships, and a fear of rejection and being left alone," and approach affiliation is "a concern with the establishment of 'love' relationships" (Boyatzis, 1973, p. 270). Individuals high on avoidance affiliation correspond to those with a need for "D-love (deficiency-love, love need, selfish love)" described by Maslow (1973, p. 249). The underlying motivation of these individuals' concern for others is to gain others' approval, to demonstrate their importance to others, and to develop their own self-worth. In essence, "their strongest drive is to be liked" (McClelland & Burnham, 1995, p. 128). Individuals high on approach affiliation are similar to those with a need for "B-love

(love for the Being of another person, unneeded love, unselfish love)" described by Maslow (1973, p. 249). The approach-affiliation individuals are motivated primarily by a genuine interest in others.

In the organizational context, Boyatzis (1982) viewed avoidance affiliation as "affiliative assurance," and approach affiliation as "affiliative interest." Individuals high on affiliative assurance emphasize relationships to protect themselves. It has its origin in the individuals' sense of insecurity and manifests itself in noninterfering and easy-to-get-along behaviors even when the job situation demands otherwise. For example, managers high on affiliative assurance are reluctant to give negative feedback to their subordinates. They yield to employee requests because they do not want to incur the employees' displeasure and they do so without regard to the effect of their behavior on the need for equity, due process, and order in the workplace. The interpersonal relations motivated by affiliative assurance produce low employee morale and a defensive feeling, which invariably "leaves employees feeling weak, irresponsible, and without a sense of what might happen next, of where they stand in relation to their manager, or even of what they ought to be doing" (McClelland & Burnham, 1995, p. 129).

On the other hand, individuals high on affiliative interest emphasize relationships in a manner that is consistent with the demands of the job tasks. It has its origin in the individuals' recognition that uncertainty pervades the workplace, and affiliative interest manifests itself in helpful but task-oriented interventions, which demonstrate a high degree of interpersonal competence. Managers who are high on affiliative interest relate to others with the full recognition that they are individual persons with ideas and resources and that they are partners in the problem-solving and related activities necessary for attaining task objectives (Moment & Zaleznik, cited in Litwin & Stringer, 1968). Consequently, supportive feelings permeate the interpersonal relations motivated by affiliative interest.

In the light of the preceding discussion, it is clear that the motivation of organizational leaders who are high on affiliative assurance is not only incompatible with the motivation that underlies moral altruism but is also diametrically opposed to it. On the other hand, the motivation of organizational leaders who are high on affiliative interest is consistent with and conducive to motivation underlying moral altruism. The success or effectiveness of leaders who are high on affiliative interest relative to those high on affiliative assurance highlights the fact that the affiliative-interest motivation exhibits to a considerable degree the underlying altruistic motive.

When one thinks of a leader, the notion that immediately comes to mind is "power." Undeniably, the power motivation or a high need for power has driven many a leader. Power, particularly in a democracy, has a very unfavorable press. The very mention of the word seems to evoke images of ruthless oppression and devious manipulation of human beings. It is, therefore, not surprising if the need for power seems as remote from the altruistic motive or behavior as night is from day. However, a closer examination of this phenomenon reveals that there are, similar to the affiliation motivation, two types of power motivations. In one case, the leader is motivated by power for personal aggrandizement; in the other case, the leader is motivated by the power to serve the purpose of the institution. McClelland and Burnham (1995) term the former as the *personal power need* and the latter as the *institutional power need.*

Before we proceed further with the discussion, it is useful to note the difference between personal and institutional power needs, as suggested by McClelland and his associates, and the concepts of personal and position *power bases,* derived from French and Raven's (1959) work on bases or sources of power referred to in Chapter 2. The need for power—be it personal or institutional—triggers or motivates the leader to exercise influence or control over the followers. The leader's power base—be it personal or position—becomes the source of the resources that the leader can draw on to exercise influence or control over the followers. Thus, the need for power provides the motivation for the exercise of influence, whereas the power base is the means that will be used for this purpose. In a sense, the need for power explains why influence or control is exercised, and the power base explains how it is exercised. The impact of these concepts on understanding leader behavior is quite significant. To exercise influence over their followers, leaders who are high in personal power need are likely to use more often their position power base—that is, the use of resources such as rights of one's office, ability to exercise coercion, and control over rewards. On the other hand, leaders who are high in the institutional power need are likely to influence their followers more often by the use of their personal power base—that is, the expertise or attraction as perceived by the followers.

We now return to the discussion of power motivation and its relation to moral altruism. Individuals high on personal power need are preoccupied with their own interests and concerns. In the organizational context, such self-interest is pursued even at the cost of the organization's welfare and effectiveness. When power is exercised in this manner, the leader demands and expects followers' loyalty and efforts to be directed toward the achievement of the leader's personal goals. For this purpose, the leaders tend to draw on the resources of their position power base. The personal power need of the leader would seem to be rooted in a deep-seated sense of personal insecurity, which manifests itself in dictatorial forms of behavior and defensive feelings in relations with the followers. These leaders, insensitive to the needs of their followers, expect the followers' unquestioning obedience to and compliance with their authority and decisions (Howell & Avolio, 1992).

On the other hand, the dominant preoccupation of individuals high on institutional power need is the interests of the organization and its members. Such individuals subordinate their personal or self-interest to that of the organization, which then becomes the sole reason for their desire to influence and control others. Leaders who are high on institutional power motivation emphasize orderliness, discipline, and task structure primarily to ensure the accomplishment of the organization's objectives. For this purpose, they draw primarily on the resources of their personal power base—that is, expertise or attraction as perceived by the followers. When they are required to use rewards and sanctions as means of control and influence, they do so impartially and equitably.

Contrary to the personal power need, the institutional power need is derived from the leader's identification with and commitment to the organization's objectives and interests. For this reason, power becomes the vehicle to serve the needs of the organization and its members. It is manifested in behaviors and feelings that serve to help and support the followers in accomplishing their tasks. Furthermore, being aware of their need to remedy the inadequacies in their competencies and abilities, the institutional power need makes leaders not only establish open communication with their followers but also create a climate in which followers are encouraged to provide suggestions and criticisms of the leader's decisions and actions (Howell & Avolio, 1992).

The discussion of the personal power need relative to the institutional power need suggests that personal power need clearly places the interests of self before that of others, and might even be at considerable cost to others; personal power need is the antithesis of altruism. On the other hand, the institutional power need places the interest of others before and might even be at the cost to self. As McClelland and Burnham (1995) observed, on the basis of their data from stories written by managers:

> The good manager's power motivation is not oriented toward personal aggrandizement but toward the institution he or she serves. . . . If a high

power-motive score is balanced by high inhibition, stories about power tend to be altruistic. That is, the heroes in the story exercise power on behalf of someone else . . . as distinguished from the concern for personal power, which is characteristic of individuals whose stories are loaded with power imagery but show no sign of inhibition or self-control. (p. 129)

In a retrospective commentary, 20 years later, McClelland (1995) states: "Indeed, such motivational characteristics continually emerge as what separates world-class managers from mediocre ones" (p. 139). Because the institutional power need manifests the altruistic motive, we can infer that leaders high on institutional power need are more likely to be effective than those high on personal power need.

The need for achievement or the achievement motive (McClelland, 1961) is one of the key elements to understanding leadership behaviors. Individuals high on the achievement motive derive satisfaction from achieving their goals, as well as from their relentless efforts in pursuit of achievement almost as an end in itself. They assume a high degree of personal responsibility but also tend to be self-oriented in that they view organizational resources and support primarily in terms of their own objectives. Similar to the affiliation and power needs, discussed previously, individuals high on the need for achievement might be motivated either by "personal achievement" or by "social achievement" (Mehta, 1994). Leaders driven by personal achievement motives are more likely to engage in behaviors that benefit self rather than others; "because they focus on personal improvement and doing things better by themselves, achievement-motivated people want to do things themselves" (McClelland & Burnham, 1995, p. 126).

On the other hand, leaders driven by the social achievement motive show a concern for others and initiate efforts "in terms of articulation of individual and collective capability, concern for a better quality of life and need to engage in meaningful organizational and social action in order to influence the environment" (Mehta, 1994, p. 171). Thus, leaders motivated by social achievement would generally tend toward efforts that primarily benefited others. However, leaders motivated by personal achievement could also engage in efforts that benefit others when the objective of their efforts also included the interests of others. For example, when leaders engage in self-development the objective might be viewed as personal achievement. However, if the ultimate objective of the leader is to prepare him- or herself to better serve the followers, then such achievement motivation would be congruent with the altruistic

Table 3.1 Two Contrasting Leadership Motive Patterns

	Underlying Motive	
	Altruistic (intent to benefit others)	Egotistic (intent to benefit self)
Operative needs	Affiliative interest	Affiliative assurance
	Institutional power	Personal power
	Social achievement	Personal achievement
	Self-discipline/self-development	Self-aggrandizement
Influence strategy	Empowerment	Control
	Referent and expert power base	Legal, coercive, and reward power base
Leadership effectiveness	High	Low

motive. In fact, it is not uncommon for effective charismatic leaders motivated by altruism to pay attention to continuous self-improvement or self-development, which enables them to better perform the several behaviors in the leadership process.

To summarize, as indicated in Chapter 2, leadership is both a relational and a followers' attribution phenomenon. Leadership behaviors are identified always in the context of the leader-follower interaction and never in isolation of each other. Consequently, the motivation underlying leader behaviors can be characterized either as altruistic or egotistic. The altruistic motivation of a leader manifests itself at the operative level in terms of affiliative interest, institutional power need, self-discipline or self-development, and social achievement needs. The egotistic motivation of a leader, on the other hand, expresses itself in affiliative assurance, personal power need, and personal achievement chiefly in terms of self-aggrandizement. These differences are summarized in Table 3.1. We also see from this table that leaders with an altruistic motivation influence followers through the strategies of empowerment and the use of expertise and attraction to their followers, whereas leaders with an egotistic motivation influence followers through control strategies and the use of legal means, coercion, and rewards and sanctions. The leadership influence strategies and processes have been referred to and described in this and in previous chapters; their ethical or moral implications will be explored in detail in the next chapter.

◪ CONCLUSION

The charismatic leadership role is effective when the leader behaviors are motivated by the altruistic motive. At any given point in time, it is possible for the charismatic leader to be motivated by one or more needs such as the needs for affiliation, power, and achievement. However, regardless of the need that operates as the motive, the leader's effectiveness will ultimately depend on whether the behavior manifested by that need is a reflection of and is guided by the overarching altruistic need.

4

Ethical Dimensions of
Leadership Influence Processes

A leader performs behaviors to influence the followers. The leadership phenomenon can, thus, be approached from the point of view of the leader's behaviors. What behaviors are typical of effective leaders? Why do leaders perform these behaviors? Answers to these questions provide information on leadership role behaviors and the motives that initiate, direct, and energize these behaviors. This approach to leadership focuses on the leadership phenomenon as a leader-centered construct. It emphasizes the leader's motivational dispositions that trigger and sustain leadership role behaviors. However, the leader's behaviors are designed to influence the followers' values, attitudes, and behaviors. This aspect of the leader role behavior provides the basis of another approach to understanding leadership, which is to view it as a social influence process. This approach allows us to explore the psychological underpinnings or explanations of the influence process involved in leader-follower relationships. The focus on the influence processes highlights the leadership phenomenon as a relational construct. The leader-centered and the relational approaches are, of course, not mutually exclusive, but complementary. Therefore, both approaches become necessary for a sound and proper understanding of leadership.

The previous chapter examined the motivational dynamics underlying behaviors that are typical of leadership roles. We saw that although the overt behaviors exhibited by effective leaders might be seen as being motivated by needs such as affiliation, power, and achievement, nevertheless, effective leadership depends on whether these behaviors reflect the overarching altruistic need. In this chapter, we discuss the leadership influence processes and the related influence strategies. More specifically, we explore the two basic influence processes available to leaders: the transactional influence process and the transformational influence process. The various types of these influence processes have been identified and described in the discussion of the modal orientations in leadership in Chapter 2. The major thrust of the discussion in this chapter is to explore the ethical or moral dimensions of the leadership influence processes and related strategies. For this purpose, we shall first examine the nature of the influence processes and related strategies and the underlying psychological mechanics and dynamics through which the beliefs, attitudes, and behaviors of both the followers and leaders are affected.

▧ THE TRANSACTIONAL INFLUENCE PROCESS

In the transactional influence process, the leader ensures through the use of rewards and sanctions that followers perform the required behaviors and demonstrate commitment and loyalty. The transactional mode of exercising leadership influence is implicit in the major leadership roles of the people orientation or social role, the task orientation or the task role, and the participative role. What precisely are the psychological dynamics that operate in the transactional influence process? What are the effects of this process on the leader and the followers? What are the ethical or moral implications of such effects?

The psychological mechanisms and dynamics of the transactional influence process can be explained in terms of the theoretical perspectives derived from the leaders' bases of social power (French & Raven, 1959), the nature of social exchange (Blau, 1974; Hollander, 1979), and the motivational dynamics (Evans, 1970; House, 1971; Luthans & Kreitner, 1975). Implicit in these perspectives is the rationale that leaders have at their command and under their control a host of resources that are valued by followers because these resources are instrumental in satisfying the followers' salient needs. These resources or strategies, described in Chapter 2, can be summarized as contingent or non-contingent rewards and punishment, authority of office or position, expertise or specialized knowledge or innovative ideas, actions to facilitate performance, setting goals and providing feedback, opportunities to participate in decision making, and loyalty and commitment to followers.

Consequently, leaders can offer these resources to followers in exchange for the followers' compliance with the leader's demands or directives, as well as for the followers' commitment and loyalty to the leader. As demonstrated by the work of Katz and Kahn (1978), the compliance behaviors can be traced to and explained by rewards and coercive and legal power strategies of the leader. The operation of the reward and coercive strategies in inducing follower compliance is understood by the motivational process postulated by expectancy theory (Kanungo & Mendonca, 1992; Lawler, 1971). Thus, followers are motivated to perform the behaviors desired by the leaders when followers expect that certain outcomes follow the performance of the behaviors and the followers value these outcomes.

In the reward strategy, the outcomes expected by the followers are the variety of rewards under the leader's control. Because followers value these rewards and will receive them only on performance of the behaviors desired by the leaders, the followers are motivated to perform these behaviors. The coercive strategy operates in a similar manner except that the followers avoid the undesired behaviors. The leader is able to influence followers to desist from undesirable behaviors because followers expect certain sanctions, which they do not value, should they perform these behaviors. The fear of the sanctions, then, becomes the basis for the influence process. In the legal strategy, followers comply because their socialization—either in terms of the sociocultural context or that of the organization's internal work culture—has prepared them to recognize or perceive that the leader has legitimate authority to require that followers perform certain behaviors. The followers' socialization, thus, plays a more significant role in the explanation of the social influence process of the legal power strategy.

The key or significant aspect about these resources and strategies—more particularly, about the way these are used—is that they enable the leader to develop a quid pro quo relationship with his or her followers. The objective of such a relationship would seem to be nothing more than that the followers should comply with the leader's goals, objectives, and directives. There is clearly no intention or desire on the part of leaders who adopt the transactional influence process to bring about a change in the individuals' attitudes or values or to facilitate the identification with or the internalization of the organization's mission and norms; neither do leaders seek to promote the growth and development of the followers.

The focus of the transactional influence process is solely on the leader's objectives, needs, and concerns. It is, therefore, not surprising if the effectiveness of the transactional influence mode is limited to the motivational "life span" of the various commodities or strategies that are used. The transactional influence process has serious ethical and moral implications, which we examine from the point of view of the followers, the organization, and the leader. This approach to exercising social influence tends to regard followers, at best, as providers of knowledge, abilities, skills, and efforts that the leaders need to accomplish their own objectives. At worst, it views followers as mere instruments or appendages of machines, which can be traded so long as the price is right. There is no consideration in the transactional influence process of the followers' needs and aspirations. It also does not provide them with an opportunity and the means to identify with and internalize the idealized vision formulated by the leaders for the organization. Consequently, it offends the dignity of the human person; it also frustrates the basic human need of maintaining self-worth and, as a result, causes much psychological and sometimes physical harm to employees (Sashkin, 1984).

In organizations where the transactional influence process prevails, followers will soon cease to experience dignity, meaning, and community so essential for the growth of both the organization and its members. In addition, such a process can lead to an inefficient deployment of the organization's resources for several reasons. First, leaders who use the transactional influence process are more likely to focus on the status quo—that is, to attend to the routine, day-to-day caretaker activities of the organization. Leaders generally find such a focus to be more convenient because it does not require them to exert the effort and experience the insecurity, uncertainty, and risks associated with change in the status quo. Nevertheless, the organization and its various stakeholders, including its members and the community in which it operates, are deprived of the benefits that accrue from strategies and actions to remedy the deficiencies in the status quo and to assess and exploit the opportunities that abound in the environment.

Second, there is the possibility that the transactional influence process can stem from the leader's operative motives of affiliative assurance, personal power, or personal achievement. The ethical implications of behaviors prompted by these motives have been fully discussed in the previous chapter.

It is useful to recognize that such motives of their leaders are readily transparent to the followers. As a result, the message to followers might be that the end justifies the means, and the leader's behavior in accord with this principle might serve as a role model and thereby lead to similar unethical behavior by the followers. Even if it does not, they will certainly not be inspired to function in a manner that serves the best interests of the organization. The third reason for the inefficient deployment of organizational resources results from the effects of leaders who do not function as role models for followers. Through the transactional influence process, they communicate to followers the message that the followers either do not have a significant role to play or that they do not have the capacity to make a meaningful contribution. The organization is, thus, deprived of the enormous resources of its members—their knowledge, skills, abilities, innovative ideas and efforts, commitment, and loyalty—which remain untapped.

When we consider the moral implications of the transactional influence process from the point of view of the leader, we must recognize that this approach is not conducive to the development of the organization's moral environment, which is a crucial responsibility of organizational leaders. Such an approach, as mentioned earlier, could create a climate that breeds dysfunctional norms and values that lead to conflict rather than cooperation among individuals and between departments because each now places its own interests before those of others without any regard to the superordinate interests of the organization, and to the organization's responsibilities and obligations to its external stakeholders. In the transactional influence mode, the exercise of power, as noted earlier, is primarily to serve the interests of the leader rather than those of the followers. Hence, it has the potential to severely impair the leader's eventual effectiveness because, as Lord Acton observed: "Power tends to corrupt and absolute power corrupts absolutely" (quoted in Bartlett, 1968, p. 750a).

▧ THE TRANSFORMATIONAL INFLUENCE PROCESS

In the transformational influence process, the leader works to bring about a change in the followers' attitudes and values as he or she moves the organization toward its future goals. In this process, leaders also use resources, including rewards and sanctions, that are at their disposal. But the use of resources is designed for one purpose: to influence followers to internalize the goals, beliefs, and values that are inherent in the vision. The transformational mode of exercising leadership influence is very explicit in the charismatic leadership role. However, it is important to recognize that when the leader adopts the charismatic role, he or she does not abandon the social role, the task role, and the participative role. These roles are performed by the charismatic leader as and when necessary to realize the vision and consistent with its beliefs and values. What precisely are the psychological dynamics that operate in the transformational influence process? What are the effects of this process on the leaders and the followers? What are the ethical or moral implications of such effects?

To understand the psychological mechanisms or dynamics underlying the transformational influence process, we shall draw on the social psychological theories of influence processes (notably, French & Raven, 1959; Kelman, 1958), of influence tactics (McClelland, 1975), and of empowerment (Conger & Kanungo, 1988c; Thomas & Velthouse, 1990). However, the basic psychological dynamics that seem to operate in the transformational influence process relate to two factors: (a) the internalization by the followers of the leader's vision and (b) the enhancement of the followers' self-efficacy beliefs—that is, the belief that they are capable of working to realize the goals of the vision. The followers' compliance behaviors and their commitment and loyalty to the leader stem from these two factors. The change in the followers' attitudes and values, therefore, results essentially from the leader's empowerment of the followers.

Although the several social psychological theories of influence processes and tactics help us to understand the transformational influence effects in leadership, the leader's empowerment strategies and the resulting empowering experience of the followers seem to be critical ingredients to the success of the transformational influence process. As will be seen from the sections that follow, it is implicit and, in fact, inherent to the charismatic leadership process described in Chapter 2. It will be recalled from that description that the charismatic leadership process consists of three stages with a set of behaviors in each stage. The three stages are (a) evaluation of the status quo, (b) formulation of organizational goals, and (c) the means to achieve. We shall consider how the transformational influence process is carried out through the activities in each stage.

In the first stage—evaluation of the status quo—the critical leader behaviors are the assessment of the environment, which includes a careful and thorough analysis of the available resources, opportunities, and constraints and of followers' needs and aspirations. It also includes a recognition of the deficiencies in the status quo, particularly in the context of the available opportunities and of followers' needs. The information gathered from such an environmental assessment becomes the foundation for leader activities and behaviors in the next stage of the charismatic leadership process. However, it is important to recognize that right from the beginning, the leader's focus is not on his or her own self or interests, but on others—the interests, needs, and aspirations of the organization and its members; the deficiencies in the status quo that impede the fulfillment of these needs; and the realization of these interests and aspirations. This focus on the other rather than on the self is a significant, if not the key, element in preparing a climate that is conducive to change in the followers' attitudes and values.

Following the first stage, the predominant activity and behavior in the second stage relates to the formulation and articulation of the vision. Motivated by the desire to remedy the deficiencies in the status quo and to seize on the opportunities that would benefit the organization and its members, the leader formulates a vision that has three important characteristics: It is *discrepant* from the status quo, *idealized*, and *shared* by the followers. Critical to the effectiveness of the transformational influence process is an idealized and shared vision. When leaders formulate an idealized vision that represents a state of profound consciousness, leaders are enabled to identify with and commit themselves to achieve the vision. This process of the leader's identification and commitment and the exertion of efforts to realize the vision directly contribute to the leader's self-development and self-actualization. Such a self-transformation that the leaders undergo then becomes the model that inspires the followers to undergo a similar inner transformation.

It is necessary to recognize that the charismatic leader's self-transformation, which triggers the transformational influence process, is more than the satisfaction of the leader's need for achievement. It has a spiritual quality that transcends the mere mundane or material sense of self-development in terms of the acquisition of some skills or attainment of an objective. The analysis of self-identity in terms of Roland's (1988) conceptualization of self may be used here to further emphasize the point that the self-transformation of charismatic leaders has indeed a spiritual component. Roland suggests that self-identity can be described as the basic inner psychological organization that enables us to develop internalized worldviews. Because the inner psychological organizations differ from person to person, our self-identities along with our internalized worldviews also differ, resulting in the profound differences in meanings we attach to our everyday experiences and relationships. Roland (1988) asserts that there are three types of "overarching or superordinate organizations of the self: the familial self, the individualized self, and the spiritual self" (p. 6). Each individual has the potential to develop self-identity along each of these dimensions of human experience.

The individualized self is characterized by an emphasis on the self-contained, competitive, individualistic "I-ness," autonomous functioning, inner separateness, contractual, and egalitarian relationships. This is the predominant mode of self-identity in North American societies. The familial self is characterized by "symbiosis-reciprocity" that involves collectivistic orientation, a sense of "we-ness," emotional intimacy with the in-group members, interdependence, and reciprocal relationships. This is the predominant mode of self-identity in Eastern societies such as in India, China, and Japan. The individualized and the familial selves are similar to the constructs of individualism-collectivism suggested by Hofstede (1980) and Triandis (1988). The third type of self that Roland postulates is the spiritual self. The spiritual self is characterized by a realization of the inner virtues and strengths, the spiritual reality or the ideals that the self tries to attain. For a person with a spiritual self-identity, "the fundamental goal of all relationships and living is the gradual self-transformation toward finer and subtler qualities and refined aspects of power in the quest for self-realization" (Roland, 1988, p. 294).

This mode of self-identity is often observed in Eastern societies such as in India and Japan, but is somewhat rare in North America. In the highly individualistic culture of North America, the existence of the spiritual dimension of human experience is often ignored or treated reductively as an aberration of the normal experience of the mundane. And yet, the spiritual self-identity is precisely what characterizes the inner psychological worldviews of the charismatic leaders. Their identification and commitment to idealized values, their efforts to develop finer and subtler qualities in themselves, their own inner self-transformation, and their missionary zeal to bring about similar transformation in others are all reflections of their spiritual self-identity. Of course, charismatic leaders' missionary zeal needs to be distinguished from that of the irrational, fanatical zealots who stop at nothing to thrust their views and ideals on the followers. The distinction is that the charismatic leader's vision is *shared* by the followers, and it is for this reason that the transformational influence process ensures that charismatic leadership is more enduring and more effective.

The articulation of the vision is an equally important behavioral component of the second stage. The formulation of the vision, although critical, remains an academic exercise unless it is communicated to the followers. As stated earlier, the contents of the vision are the nature of the status quo and its shortcomings, the beneficial opportunities that exist, and how the status quo prevents the organization and its members from availing themselves of these opportunities; the nature of the vision and how, when realized, it will remedy the existing deficiencies and become the most effective vehicle to bring about the fulfillment of the hopes of the followers; and, finally, the plan of action that provides the broad framework of strategies that are necessary to translate the vision into reality. The mode of communication is as important as the contents of the vision, hence, the need for effective articulation.

However, the articulation of the vision must convey the central idea that the vision is more than a utopian view of the future but an attainable goal. Articulation, thus, becomes the expression of the most profound convictions and beliefs of the leader. The communication of these convictions and beliefs, in practical terms, means that the leader evokes in followers the same passion and zeal that the leader has for the vision. For this purpose, the articulation of the vision will emphasize the attainability of the vision and, more important, the leader's convictions that the followers have the capability, resources, and courage to do what is necessary to attain the vision. In this process, leaders will also draw attention to their own expertise, which testifies to their capability, and their willingness to work with and support their followers' efforts.

The effects of the leader's formulation and articulation of the vision, as just described, is to engender in followers trust in the leader. The followers' trust is earned not just by inspirational articulation of the vision—although this is necessary. It is not developed by the statement of the vision and of the leader's expertise in glowing and convincing terms—although this is also necessary. The followers begin to trust their leader when they perceive, beyond any doubt, that their leader is unflinchingly dedicated to the vision and is willing to work toward it even at the risk of considerable personal cost and sacrifice. Although the first two stages of the charismatic leadership process explain the psychological dynamics of the transformational influence process, it is really the third stage—the actual activities and behaviors to achieve the vision—that provides a complete understanding of the effectiveness of the transformational influence process. The charismatic leader activities and behaviors in this stage that are the crux of the transformational influence process are the empowerment strategies, the strategy relating to outcomes or opportunities provided to followers, and the mode of exercising leadership power. We examine each of these in some detail.

The Empowerment Strategies

In the fields of industrial sociology and organizational behavior, most theorists have dealt with "empowerment" as a set of managerial techniques without paying sufficient attention to the nature and processes underlying the construct. This may have created a management ethos regarding some techniques to overcome worker alienation, but this focus has not adequately increased our understanding of the notion of empowerment and the theoretical and moral rationale for related delineation practices. For example, until the recent work of Conger and Kanungo (1988c), most scholars assumed that empowerment is the same as managers delegating or sharing power with subordinates. Viewing this traditional approach to empowerment as too limiting, Conger and Kanungo (1988c) have argued for an alternate interpretation and have identified a number of contexts most appropriate for empowerment practices within organizations. The following section briefly describes the analysis of Conger and Kanungo of the empowerment process. Their analysis demonstrates that empowerment strategies are at the core of the transformational influence leadership process.

Conger and Kanungo (1988c) proposed that empowerment can be viewed in two different ways: as a relational and as a motivational construct. If one considers empowerment as a relational construct, then one must understand it in terms of the relational dynamics of power sharing among workers and management. Thus, empowerment becomes the process by which management gives away or shares power with workers. Power, in this context, is interpreted as the possession of formal authority or control over organizational resources. The emphasis is primarily on the notion of sharing authority and resources. Burke's (1986) position is representative in this regard: "To empower, implies the granting of power—delegation of authority" (p. 51). *Merriam Webster's Dictionary* similarly describes the verb *to empower* as "to authorize or delegate or give legal power to someone." In the organizational literature, this idea of delegation and the decentralization of decision-making power is central to the empowerment notion (Burke, 1986; Kanter, 1983).

As a result, management practitioners equate empowerment with participative management techniques such as management by objectives (MBO),
quality circles, and goal setting by subordinates as the means of sharing power
or delegating authority (Likert, 1961, 1967; McGregor, 1960). However, this
line of reasoning does not adequately address the nature of empowerment as
experienced by workers because (a) it assumes that these are the only techniques that will automatically empower the workers; (b) it does not explore the
psychological mechanisms underlying empowerment; (c) the effects of these
techniques are assumed to be the same as the effects of an empowering
experience; and (d) it does not consider the moral justification for these
techniques, nor does it consider whether the conflict and tension, which might
be generated by the techniques, are morally defensible.

The second way of interpreting empowerment as a motivational construct
stems from the social psychological literature. Here empowerment is used as a
motivational and/or expectancy belief state internal to individuals. For instance, individuals are assumed to have a need for power (McClelland, 1975)
where power connotes an internal urge to influence and control other people.
A related but more inclusive disposition to control and cope with life events
has also been proposed by several psychologists dealing with the issues of
primary/secondary control (Rothbaum, Weisz, & Snyder, 1982), internal/
external locus of control (Rotter, 1966), and learned helplessness (Abramson,
Garber, & Seligman, 1980). Individuals feel empowered when they perceive
that they can adequately cope with events, situations, and/or the people they
confront. On the other hand, individuals feel powerless when they believe that
they are unable to cope with the physical and social demands of the environment.

Empowerment in this motivational sense also refers to a belief in self-
determination (Deci, 1975) or a belief in personal self-efficacy (Bandura, 1986)
as the individual copes with environmental demands. Any organizational
strategy or technique that strengthens this self-determination or self-efficacy
belief of workers will tend to make them feel empowered at work and, consequently, unalienated. Conversely, any strategy that weakens their self-determination or self-efficacy belief will increase their sense of personal powerlessness
or alienation in relation to the work context. In fact, the *Concise Oxford English
Dictionary* defines the verb *empower* as "to enable." In contrast to the earlier
definition of empowerment as delegation (of authority and resource sharing),
the connotation of enabling implies motivation through the enhancement of
one's personal efficacy and ability to cope with environmental demands.

In view of the conceptual difficulties raised in connection with empowerment as a relational construct, Conger and Kanungo (1988c) proposed that empowerment be viewed as a motivational construct—meaning "to enable" rather than simply "to delegate." Enabling implies the creation of conditions that heighten the motivation for task accomplishment through the development of a strong sense of personal efficacy. The moral justification for empowerment strategies lies in viewing empowerment as an enabling, rather than as a delegating, process. Alienation, or a sense of powerlessness, cripples the workers by "disabling" them; empowerment, or an enhancement of self-efficacy, develops workers by enabling them. Managerial practices that cripple workers' potential are morally wrong, but empowerment practices that develop workers' potential are ethical imperatives, more fully discussed in a later section.

Empowerment as an unalienating strategy becomes critical when subordinates feel powerless and self-estranged. Thus, it is important to identify conditions within organizations (structures and processes) that foster these variants of alienation among subordinates. Once the antecedent conditions of alienation are identified, empowerment strategies and interventions can then be used to remove these conditions or to minimize their disabling effects. However, just the removal of external conditions (through restructuring, altering policies, redesigning jobs, etc.) is neither always possible nor sufficient to result in the workers experiencing empowerment, unless the strategies and interventions directly provide them with information that enhances their personal efficacy. Bandura (1986) suggests several sources from which individuals directly receive information about their personal efficacy. These sources are good guides for developing the appropriate empowerment strategies.

Conger and Kanungo (1988c) have proposed a five-stage model of the empowerment process that might help leaders develop effective empowerment strategies. The first stage is the diagnosis of conditions within the organization that are responsible for the feelings of the powerlessness types of alienation among organizational members and attempts to modify or eliminate these conditions. An extensive list of such contextual conditions has been prepared by Conger and Kanungo (1988c) as a diagnostic checklist. Such a diagnosis prepares leaders for Stage 2, the use of empowerment strategies such as participative management, goal setting, and modeling. The employment of these strategies is aimed at not only removing some of the external conditions responsible for alienation but, more important, at providing followers with the self-efficacy information, which is discussed in Stage 3.

A number of leadership practices that have the potential to heighten a sense of self-efficacy among followers can be identified. At an interpersonal level, leaders should express confidence in followers accompanied by high performance expectations (Burke, 1986; House, 1988b; Neilsen, 1986), encourage participation in decision making (Block, 1987; Burke, 1986; House, 1988b; Kanter, 1979; Neilsen, 1986; Strauss, 1977), provide autonomy from bureaucratic constraint (Block, 1987; House, 1988b; Kanter, 1979), and set inspirational and/or meaningful goals (Block, 1987; Burke, 1986; Conger & Kanungo, 1987; McClelland, 1975; Tichy & Devanna, 1986).

To be effective, the empowerment practices, outlined above, must also directly provide information to followers about their personal efficacy, as required by Stage 3 of the model. Bandura (1986) identified four sources of such information: enactive attainment, vicarious experience, verbal persuasion, and emotional arousal state. Information in personal efficacy through enactive attainment refers to an individual's authentic mastery experience directly related to the job. When followers perform complex tasks or are given more responsibility in their jobs, participate in goal setting or decision making, and so on, they have the opportunity to test their efficacy.

Sashkin (1984) has advocated, as ethical imperatives, participation in four areas such as setting goals, making decisions, solving problems, and making changes in organizations as ethical imperatives. The reasons for Sashkin's advocacy lie not in the opportunity for participation per se, but rather in the personal efficacy information that such participation provides through enactive attainment. Participation in goal setting increases the followers' goal acceptance and commitment (Locke & Latham, 1984) because it increases the followers' understanding of what their tasks are and how to go about accomplishing the tasks and, as a result, their confidence in their ability to attain the goal. Any kind of initial success experience in handling tasks and various training experiences in acquiring new skills can make the followers feel more capable and, therefore, empowered.

The feeling of being empowered can also come from vicarious experiences of observing others perform successfully on the job. Such modeling techniques can often be used to empower followers. Very often the leader's exemplary behaviors empower followers to believe that they can behave in a like manner, or at least can achieve some improvement in their performance (Conger & Kanungo, 1987). Words of encouragement, verbal feedback, and other forms of social persuasion can be used by leaders to empower followers and by followers to empower their peers. Finally, the personal competence expectations are affected by the emotional arousal state of the individual. Empowerment techniques and strategies that reduce stress and provide emotional support to followers and that create a supportive and trusting group atmosphere (Neilsen, 1986) can be more effective in strengthening self-efficacy beliefs.

The final two stages of the empowerment process suggested by Conger and Kanungo (1988c) describe the nature of empowering experience and its behavioral effects. As a result of receiving self-efficacy information from the leadership practices outlined above, followers feel empowered, that is, the belief in their own capabilities is strengthened, or the belief in their powerlessness is weakened. The behavioral effect of empowerment as an unalienating experience results in followers both initiating and persevering in work behavior, and it thereby makes the quality of their work life more rich, active, and dynamic. As Bandura (1977) points out:

> The strength of people's conviction in their own effectiveness is likely to affect whether they would even try to cope with given situations. . . . They get involved in activities and behave assuredly when they judge themselves capable of handling situations that would otherwise be intimidating. . . . Efficacy expectations determine how much effort people will expend and how long they will persist in the face of obstacles and aversive experiences. (pp. 193-194)

Self-assured followers tend to be more satisfied, be more productive, and contribute more to the organization and the society at large.

Strategy Relating to Outcomes and Opportunities

The empowerment strategy should flow naturally from an organizational culture and philosophy congruent with values and norms that support and are consistent with the empowerment of followers. These values and norms are self-determination, collaboration rather than conflict or competition, high performance standards and expectations, nondiscrimination, and meritocracy (House, 1988a). For this purpose, the reward systems should be designed to emphasize innovative performance as well as high performance levels. Critical to the success of the reward system design is that the rewards are valued by followers and are contingent on task performance and related behaviors that followers see as appropriate and conducive to the realization of the established vision and goals (Kanter, 1979; Kanungo, 1987). Furthermore, the design and administration of the reward system should be conducted in a fair and equitable manner.

When leaders are not concerned with or are indifferent to procedural justice, when they do not administer rewards fairly but in an arbitrary or capricious way—as is often the case when leaders are influenced by the ingratiating behaviors of some followers—then followers experience dissatisfaction with leaders' decisions. Such decisions suggest a rather patronizing attitude of the leader toward the followers. The uncertainty and inequity of outcomes that result from the leader's patronizing attitude and behaviors lead to several undesirable consequences. They reduce the followers' beliefs that their efforts to realize the vision will lead to the expected beneficial outcomes. They cause the leaders to lose credibility in the eyes of the followers, which adversely affects followers' trust and confidence in the vision. Finally, they reduce the followers' motivation to exert the needed effort to work toward the attainment of the vision.

The empowerment of followers is also greatly enhanced when leaders exercise the expert and referent power strategies (French & Raven, 1959). In these strategies, the source of the transformational influence is not the organization, but the leaders themselves. The leader's expert power is effective in the influence process because followers perceive their leader to possess the knowledge, abilities, and expertise that followers can draw on and that they see to be necessary for the attainment of the vision. The followers' perception that their leader possesses the needed expertise makes the leader credible and trustworthy. Similar to the expert power, the leader's referent power also lies in the followers' perceptions of the leader's commitment to their welfare. In this case too it is not enough that leaders have certain personal qualities and characteristics, however noble or endearing these might be. The leader's influence on followers is derived from the fact that followers perceive the leader's efforts to be selfless and their intent to be altruistic. As a result of such perceptions, the followers are attracted to and identify with the leader.

Although the strategies relating to outcomes and opportunities have been discussed separately from the empowerment strategies, their effects on the followers are the same: All these strategies contribute to transforming the self-efficacy beliefs of the followers. Through these strategies, followers are enabled to perform well beyond the organization's expectations (Bass, 1985). The preceding discussion explored the nature of the psychological dynamics that explain the transformational influence processes of leadership. We conclude with an examination of the processes of attitudinal change proposed by Kelman (1958). His formulation provides a fuller understanding of the psychological dynamics at work in both the transactional and transformational influence processes of leadership. It also provides a base from which to examine the moral or ethical dimensions of leadership influence processes.

According to Kelman (1958), there are three processes of attitude change: compliance, identification, and internalization. Thus, in compliance, "an individual accepts influence . . . adopts the induced behavior—not because he believes in its content but because he expects to gain specific rewards or approval and avoid specific punishments or disapproval by conforming" (Kelman, 1958, p. 53). The followers' compliance behavior depends on the leader's control of rewards and punishment and, furthermore, on the leader's continuous monitoring of the followers' behavior. The change in the followers is temporary and superficial. It does not extend to change in the followers' attitudes, beliefs, and values. As indicated previously, it is typical of the transactional influence process of leadership.

The next change relates to identification, which occurs when "an individual accepts influence because he wants to establish or maintain a satisfying self-defining relationship to another person. . . . The individual actually believes in the responses which he adopts through identification, but their specific content is more or less irrelevant" (Kelman, 1958, p. 53). The followers are attracted to the leader "as a person"—the leader's qualities, characteristics, reputation, and so on, which might be analogous to "hero-worship." But it is important to note that the attraction is not based on the leader's control over rewards and sanctions. Of course, the leader's influence will operate so long as the attraction from the followers continues. In the internalization process of attitude change, the "individual accepts influence because the content of the induced behavior—the ideas and actions of which it is composed—is intrinsically rewarding . . . because it is congruent with his value system" (Kelman, 1958, p. 53). In the context of the leader-follower interaction, the leader's vision, values, and goals will be the key ingredients in the leadership influence process provided that followers subscribe to the leader's vision and values and adopt the related norms.

The identification process describes the followers' change of attitude toward the leader, who is now no longer viewed as a potentially useful person with valued resources that can satisfy the followers' needs, or with the power to enforce compliance with the leader's wishes. Instead, the followers are attracted to the leader, who is held in awe and admired and adored as a "hero" whose life is worthy of emulation. The internalization process describes a more fundamental or profound change that leadership influence brings about in the followers. This change is the transformation of the followers' innermost core values and goals. With very rare exceptions, it is unlikely that the identification and internalization processes would occur simultaneously. Generally, the leader's use of empowerment strategies would first result in the followers' identification with the leader, and then, over time, in their internalization of the values and the idealized vision professed by the leader.

The identification and internalization processes of attitude change help us to understand the nature and success of the transformational influence processes of leadership. These processes also underscore the significance and role of empowerment and related strategies in the transformational influence processes of leadership. The focus of these strategies is on the followers rather than on the leader, and followers clearly understand the thrust of the leader's message to be that "I will attend to your personal growth and competence regardless of the personal cost and sacrifice to me."

◪ ETHICAL IMPLICATIONS OF THE TRANSACTIONAL AND TRANSFORMATIONAL INFLUENCE PROCESSES

The transformation or change in the followers' attitudes and values in the direction of the goals, beliefs, and values that are inherent in the vision is the objective of the leadership influence process. As discussed, this transformation, which occurs essentially through the identification and internalization processes of attitude change, can be brought about by the leader through either control or empowerment strategies. Although either strategy produces transformation in followers, the nature and effects of such transformation are radically different and have significant ethical implications.

The sustained use of control strategies, based on the leader's coercive, legal, or reward power base, can over a long period of time produce transformational effects in followers, changing their values and attitudes. Initially, followers identify with the transactional leader, but it is a "defensive" identification process (Freud, 1946; Mowrer, 1950). The identification serves to constantly remind the followers of the negative consequences that follow when they do not comply with the leader's directives. Such forms of identification have been observed in both children (Whiting, 1960) and adults (Bettelheim, 1943; Schein, 1958). The analogy that appropriately depicts the followers' identification with the transactional leader is that of "servile" imitation—the imitation that is proper of the slave in relation to the master on whom the slave is completely dependent.

The control strategy also influences followers to internalize the norms, values and beliefs, and attitudes of the transactional leader. But this "internalization" is more in the nature of the followers being programmed to think and behave as the leader desires—much like programmed robots. Thus, the identification and internalization processes generated by the control strategies of transactional leadership are quite effective in enforcing compliance behaviors of the followers. But it is achieved by the virtual destruction of the individual's self-worth. The control strategy is manipulative and is offensive to the dignity of the person. It reflects the leader's egotistic value orientation because it is primarily intended to benefit the self at the cost of the other. For these reasons, the transactional influence process of leadership is, objectively, unethical.

On the other hand, the empowerment strategy that is used in transformational leadership promotes the followers' attraction to the leader, who is perceived as the source of support and nurturance. In other words, the identification process originates from the self-growth orientation of the followers. Consequently, the followers identify with the leader because of their concern that failure to do so would cause them to be detached or disconnected from the leader's trust and nurturance that constitute the basis of their self-growth or development. Perhaps an appropriate analogy to depict the followers' identification with the transformational leader might be that of "filial" imitation—the imitation that is proper for and becoming to a child in relation to his or her parents. The child imitates the parents because they are perceived to be the epitome of all that is good and wise. Furthermore, as discussed previously, the internalization process fostered by the empowerment strategy allows for a free choice by followers to subscribe to the leader's vision, values, and goals and to adopt the related norms and behaviors. In fact, the whole point of the empowerment strategy is to enhance the followers' self-efficacy beliefs, which then become the foundation for their self-growth and functioning as autonomous persons.

Thus, the identification and internalization processes generated by empowerment strategies enhance the followers' self-worth and their dignity as human beings. By their very nature, empowerment strategies involve a concern for others before self, which is manifested at every stage of the charismatic leadership process, from the assessment of the environment and formulation and articulation of the vision to the means to achieve the vision. The empowerment strategy reflects the altruistic value and orientation.

In Chapter 3, we explored the basis of moral altruism. This value becomes even more crucial and pivotal when we discuss the transformational influence process, which directly involves the relationship between persons. The commandment to love one's neighbor is universal to all religious traditions. In terms of philosophical ethics, it translates into:

> The person is a being for whom the only suitable dimension is love. We are just to a person if we love him. . . . Love is not limited to excluding all behavior that reduces the person to a mere object of pleasure. It requires more; it requires the affirmation of the person as a person . . . and the sincere gift of self. . . . Man affirms himself most completely by giving of himself. (John Paul II, 1994, pp. 201-202)

The empowerment and related strategies are an ideal way for leaders to exercise ethically the social influence process of leadership. However, is there an ethical imperative for leaders to empower their followers for reasons that go well beyond the pragmatic considerations of the "bottom line"? In other words, do leaders have the moral obligation to empower their followers and, thereby, promote their growth and development even if such development means that they might leave the organization to join its competitors? This is a pertinent question, particularly in the context of work organizations where managers seek to adopt the charismatic leadership role in relation to their subordinates. To address this question, one needs to explore the human value and morality of work.

In such an exploration, one cannot escape the realization that work is inextricably bound up with human existence. To a human being, work is more than a means of earning one's livelihood. It is an essential means of self-development and of the development of society—its science, technology, and culture. It is a free, conscious act of a human being and, as a consequence, work acquires its value from the dignity of the human being as a person. Work—its content and context—should, therefore, promote rather than damage the dignity of the human being. This vision of the values of human work is often blurred, if not gravely distorted, when work is viewed in terms of social exchange theory, as a commodity that is sold by the employee in return for wages and benefits, and the employer, by virtue of his or her ownership of capital, assumes the right to regard employees as instruments in the production process. Such a view distorts the reality because even though the worker does not own the capital (technology, know-how, etc.), it is the worker who uses or operates it.

Therefore, in the production process, the worker is the primary efficient cause, whereas capital remains a mere instrument in the hands of the workers. Furthermore, the right to private property (including the right to capital) is not an absolute right. It is subject to the right that every human being has to access and use the resources of nature—the common patrimony of humanity. From this standpoint, capital (technology, know-how, etc.) is the result of the interaction (direct or indirect) between the owner's labors and the natural resources. Therefore, when workers are engaged in the production process, they are entitled to consider themselves as part owners of the capital that is employed.

These truths, so evident from humanity's historical experience, confirm the principle of the priority of labor over capital, which is acquired through work in order that it may serve work in the future. Certain specific rights flow from this principle—rights that go beyond the right to proper working conditions and remuneration. These rights include work whose content and context (including the superior-subordinate relationship) do not treat employees as "instruments" of production, but accord to them their due rights as a primary efficient cause of production, with the right and duty to take such initiatives that one would if one were self-employed. In other words, the organization must also enable its employees to preserve their awareness that they are working for "themselves," which approach alone is consistent with the dignity of the human person. As the Second Vatican Council declared:

> Just as human activity proceeds from man, so it is ordered towards man. For when a man works he not only alters things and society, he develops himself as well. He learns much, he cultivates his resources, he goes outside of himself and beyond himself. Rightly understood, this kind of growth is of greater value than any external riches which can be garnered. (1963, p. 233)

In addition to the employee rights that impose moral obligations on the manager, there are also the obligations that follow because the manager is a member of the work community and is expected to exercise a leadership role in the community. In the words of Pope John Paul II (1981), "Work bears a particular mark of man and of humanity, the mark of a person operating within a community of persons" (p. 4). The manager and his or her subordinates constitute one such community in a work organization. It seems clearly evident that the human value and morality of work creates an obligation for the manager to be responsible for the development of the members of his or her work community.

Does this moral obligation exist even when it is likely that the employee might leave the organization and join the competitor? One might be tempted to respond to this question in the affirmative because the organization might still benefit from good public relations—the very high probability that the people who were treated with dignity would tend to speak well of the organization. However, the response to this question ought to be based on an examination of the basis of the obligation. The preceding discussion makes clear that the obligation does not stem from the pragmatic considerations of the bottom line or a similar organizational interest. Rather, it flows from the consideration of human value and morality of work that, unlike the social exchange theory, does not regard employees as mere instruments in the production process. Hence, the only morally defensible limitation on this obligation would be the subordinate's capabilities and willingness to grow and develop in the job.

◩ CONCLUSION

This chapter explored the transactional and transformational leadership influence processes. As summarized in Table 4.1, there are significant contrasts between these influence processes.

The transactional leader uses the control strategy to emphasize compliance behavior by the followers. It relies on the social exchange of valued resources that leaders can draw from their reward, coercive, and legal power base. The control strategy brings about attitude change in followers through the identification and internalization process. However, the compliance by followers

Table 4.1   A Comparison of the Transactional and Transformational Leadership
Influence Processes

Leadership Influence Process	Transactional Leadership	Transformational Leadership
Strategies	Control	Empowerment
Leader objective in terms of behavioral outcomes	Emphasis on compliance behavior	Changing followers' core attitudes, beliefs, and values
Underlying psychological mechanism	Social exchange of valued resources	Increasing self-efficacy belief and self-determination
Power base	Coercive, legal, reward	Expert and referent
Attitude change process and effects	Compliance, which under excessive control, often leads to demolishing followers' self-worth and to their functioning as programmed robots	Identification and internalization leading to followers' self-growth and to their functioning as autonomous persons
Moral implication	Unethical	Ethical

often leads to self-denial and the loss of self-worth, with the result that they
might not function much differently from programmed robots. The near
destruction of the followers' self-esteem for the benefit of the leader makes the
transactional influence process highly offensive to the dignity of people; therefore, it cannot be considered to be an ethical social influence process.

On the other hand, the transformational leader's objective is to change the
followers' core attitude and values through empowerment strategies. The
followers' empowering experience increases their self-efficacy belief and their
capacity for self-determination. The source of the transformational influence
is twofold—the leader's expert power and referent power. The expert power
makes the leader credible and trustworthy to the followers; the referent power
makes the leader attractive to the followers mainly because of the leader's
selfless efforts and altruistic intent. The empowerment strategy also brings
about attitude change in followers through the identification and internalization processes. However, unlike the transactional leader, these processes are
designed by the transformational leader to increase the followers' self-growth,

enhance their self-worth, and enable them to function as autonomous persons. These effects reflect the leader's altruistic value and orientation and promote the dignity of the human person.

We can, therefore, conclude that when leaders adopt the transformational influence process mode, their leadership is more likely to be ethical, more effective, and more enduring.

5

Preparing for Ethical Leadership

A leader is best when people barely
know he exists.
Not so good when people obey and
acclaim him.
Worse when they despise him.
If you fail to honour people,
they fail to honour you.
But of a good leader,
who talks little,
when his work is done,
his aim fulfilled,
they will say "We did this ourselves!"

Lao-Tzu (quoted in Bynner, 1962, pp. 34-35)

Lao-Tzu's description of a leader aptly and succinctly makes the point that the leader's life is best epitomized by the dictum "others before self"—at all times and regardless of the cost to self. It also confirms and reinforces the discussion in the book, so far, that has advocated that effective leadership is prompted by the altruistic motive and exercised by the transformational influence mode. Clearly, charismatic leadership needs great inner strength to meet the challenging demands of the role. The question we now address is, How do managers prepare themselves for the charismatic leadership role? The sections that follow explore this question from the point of view of two different but related aspects. First is the need to recognize that the sociocultural environment in which leaders function might not be particularly conducive or receptive to altruistic behavior. For this reason, we examine the obstacles to altruism in the organizational context. Second, we discuss some of the sources that a charismatic leader might draw on to develop as a moral person possessed of inner strength and resourcefulness and to develop the moral environment of the organization to ensure that its culture might be imbued with the spirit of altruism.

▧ OBSTACLES TO ALTRUISM IN ORGANIZATIONAL CONTEXTS

A recent fax poll "Altruism in Corporate America" (Viega & Dechant, 1993) asked the question: "In the last twenty years, do you think acts of corporate altruism have increased? stayed the same? decreased?" (p. 89). This question was addressed to members of the Academy of Management's Executive Advisory Panel and of the Conference Board Council on Development, Education and Training, who were also asked to obtain responses to this question from a few other executives in their firms. The results were as follows: 52.5% said that altruism had increased, 31.7% said that it had stayed the same, and 15.8% that it had decreased. In terms of the altruism matrix discussed in Chapter 3, the responses revealed that the altruistic practices in the polled organizations were motivated, to a large extent, by "utilitarian altruism" rather than by "genuine altruism." The poll probed further to determine what might be the barriers to and facilitators of corporate altruism.

The responses identified the barriers to altruism:

- Short-term pressure for profit—"The market has a reptilian mind, it doesn't care about your values or altruism."
- Leadership and organizational culture—"Corporate leaders who do not recognize the social role of organizations as neighbors," "lack of vision . . . maintaining a shortsightedness regarding the need for some altruistic behavior."

The facilitators of corporate altruism were identified:

- Leader's values—"A true leader who has a set of personal values," "an altruistic CEO."

- If altruism is part of a "strategic vision which is well-understood." (Viega & Dechant, 1993, p. 91)

Clearly, all is not well in corporate America as far as the ethic of altruism is concerned. Nevertheless, the need for this ethic is being expressed every now and then, as the following two items show.

First, a *Time* magazine article in 1970, "The Executive as a Social Activist," asserted:

> The American businessman is being challenged to effect change within his own organization: to hire more of the poor, to stop the pollution that his company produces, to manufacture safer and more reliable products. Beyond that, he is being asked to reach more broadly into the community: to use his company's talent, capital, and organizational skill to repair the rattles in the nation's social machinery. (p. 50)

In responding to such challenges, the article noted:

> U.S. corporate leaders have begun articulating a new philosophy: that business is part of the total society and has an obligation to attack a broad range of social problems if need be in ways that temporarily retard profits. The new mood reflects much genuine altruism. (p. 50)

According to a recent newspaper report: "Some of the most powerful people in American business went back to school for two days and got a stern lecture on ethics and personal responsibility" (Flinn, 1995, p. C2). They were attending the Stanford Law School's program of workshops for corporate directors on topics such as how to respond to shareholder activism and how to avoid allegations of fraud. Arthur Levitt, chairman of the U.S. Securities and Exchange Commission, delivered the keynote address and later told reporters that corporate directors need to consider questions and issues such as:

> Are they more concerned about what they receive than what they contribute? ... If you suddenly find yourself with season tickets on the 50-yard line, you're being seduced. If you are swept off by corporate jet to meetings in Hawaii and Nassau, you're being seduced. If there's an offer to pay one board member more than the others ... chances are that director is being seduced. These are things that can—and usually do—lead to larger problems. (Flinn, 1995, p. C2)

When we read of the need for altruistic behavior in the organizational context, we are not surprised because our experience tells us that without generous doses of altruism, life and living in a society would simply be intolerable. We see that altruistic behavior surrounds our day-to-day personal, family, and social lives. As parents, we nurture children and devote ourselves to the needs and cares of the family; as citizens, we are engaged in a host of voluntary community service activities such as Boy Scouts, Girl Guides, and Meals-on-Wheels for older persons and people with disabilities. The early socialization practices in the family, school, and religious contexts inculcate and encourage such behaviors because these are considered to be the moral foundations of personality development. Because altruistic behaviors are considered vital to our moral development, many scholars have proposed a stable dispositional and motivational basis for such behavior. For instance, Murray (1938) and, later, Jackson (1967) postulated the need for nurturance as the basis of altruistic behavior. Likewise, Maslow (1967) suggested that the self-actualizing value of "goodness," when internalized, may prompt unselfish behavior. The question then is, Why is altruism ignored or neglected in the organizational context?

Although altruism as a form of prosocial behavior stemming from an intrinsic motive has been investigated in both the motivational and social psychological literature (see, e.g., Mook, 1987; Worchel et al., 1988), such behavior in organizational contexts has been neglected as a subject of serious scientific study. A cursory look at recent reviews of the research literature (e.g., House & Singh, 1987) shows no reference to altruism. Instead, management research has centered primarily on the achievement and power phenomena within organizations (McClelland, 1961, 1975; Mintzberg, 1983; Pfeffer, 1981; Winter, 1973) to the complete exclusion of examining altruistic motives and behaviors among organizational members.

Fortunately, the literature on social responsibility and business ethics has responded to the increased public criticism of business during the 1950s and 1960s for its insensitivity and neglect in areas such as environmental pollution and hazardous products. As a result, management training programs today contain courses on business ethics (Schermerhorn, Hunt, & Osborn, 1988), and during the past three decades, numerous research publications on corporate morality have appeared (Baumhart, 1968; Schmidt & Posner, 1983; Toffler, 1986). However, this literature deals only with the macrolevel issues of organizational values and their compatibility with society's moral standards. It does not deal directly with the more microlevel issues of the nature, causes, and consequences of altruistic motives and behaviors by organizational members. Nevertheless, the business ethics literature suggests indirectly, but strongly, that to achieve organizational compatibility with society's moral standards, there is a need for organizations to recognize and promote altruism among its members.

There are several reasons that might explain why altruistic behavior is ignored in business organizations. One reason might be the absence of an altruism construct in the organizational behavior literature. The other reason might be the societal norms for or expectations of the behavior of business executives. The third reason might be the cultural and historical forces that have contributed to a form of individualism that is inimical to altruistic behavior in business organizations. We explore these reasons because through an awareness of these reasons, leaders are better prepared to recognize and assess the obstacles to altruistic behaviors and to develop appropriate strategies to overcome these obstacles.

When we examine the organizational behavior literature, we find that it has identified and analyzed a variety of behaviors in the workplace that contain elements of altruistic behavior. We refer to activities such as mentoring (Levinson, 1976), Japanese management practices (Ouchi, 1981; Pascale & Athos, 1981), empowerment behaviors (Burke, 1986; Conger & Kanungo, 1988c; Kanter, 1983; Neilsen, 1986), team building (Dyer, 1977), some forms of organizational spontaneity (George & Brief, 1992), prosocial organizational behavior (Brief & Motowidlo, 1986), and citizenship behavior (Organ, 1988). These activities involve actions performed for the benefit of others but are simply designated and categorized as specific management strategies or practices rather than as a subclass of the larger category of altruism. Thus, the absence of the single, unifying construct of altruism has led organizational theorists to overlook the altruistic nature of these activities.

The second reason is the societal norms for or expectations of the behavior of business leaders. In a study of public attitudes toward altruism or helping behavior in 20 selected occupations, Rotter and Stein (1971) found executives of large companies were ranked very close to the bottom—that is, perceived as being egotistic. They fared only slightly better than used car salesmen and politicians. And in spite of differences in education and geography, four separate samples of respondents uniformly maintained that executives act in their own self-interest and help others only if they lose nothing by doing so.

Such is the stereotype of executives in large corporations. The study also revealed that members of the clergy and physicians were ranked high on altruism, showing concern for the good of others through personal sacrifice. As can be seen, there is a bias in the public mind that executives are self-centered, egotistic individuals. They and their organizations are perceived as economic entities concerned primarily with gaining material advantage for themselves. Their main objective is to make themselves and their organizations "winners" in the cutthroat competition of the free market. To win, executives are expected to protect their self-interest even if it requires harming their competitors.

Thus, managers are viewed primarily as selfish individuals devoid of moral obligations for the interests of others. This selfish nature is seen as the natural outcome of environmental demands. Just as religious and health service organizations promote altruistic behavior among clergy and physicians in the service of their clients, industrial organizations are assumed to promote competitive behavior on the part of executives to benefit themselves and their clients (shareholders, investors, etc.). These expectations have formed the social norms for executive behavior and have fostered a self-fulfilling prophecy for executives. Perhaps, guided by such norms, executives themselves have been somewhat reluctant to exhibit altruistic behavior. In the public's attitude, they have found a rational justification for their lack of altruistic concern. The spin-off effects of societal expectations might be that organizational theorists have likewise concentrated on researching executive power and achievement and have largely ignored altruism in the belief that it is less relevant to the normal functions of an executive.

The perceived irrelevance of altruistic behavior among executives was most eloquently expressed some time ago by Theodore Levitt (1958). Levitt observed that "altruism, self-denial, charity, and similar values are vital in certain walks of life. But for the most part, those virtues are alien to competitive economics" (p. 49). To emphasize his point, Levitt argued that business should never indulge in altruism unless it makes economic sense: "The governing rule in industry should be that something is good only if it pays. Otherwise it is alien and impermissible. This is the rule of capitalism" (p. 48). In contrast to certain other professions, Levitt (1958) commented that the executive

> whose only aim is personal aggrandizement and whose tactics are a vulgar combination of compulsive demagoguery and opportunistic cynicism is less dangerous than the social evangelist who, to borrow from Nietzsche, thinks of

himself as "God's ventriloquist." . . . There is nothing more corrupting than self-righteousness and nothing more intolerant than an ardent man who is convinced he is on the side of the angels. (p. 46)

The third and, we believe, the most fundamental and possibly the root cause or explanation for the neglect of or indifference to altruism in business organizations is the impact of the sociohistorical forces, which can be analyzed from both the economic and psychological perspectives. From an economic perspective, organizations are considered most efficient when the classical mechanism of a laissez-faire philosophy is at work. The work of Adam Smith (1776/1936) and, more recently, Milton Friedman (1963) advocates the notion that a free and competitive market contributes not only to the profitability of the most efficient organization but also to the good of society. Human selfishness in this context is considered divine providence. The Darwinian notion of "survival of the fittest" and Jeremy Bentham's hedonistic psychology and utilitarian moral philosophy emphasizing an "enlightened self-interest" are often considered ideological justifications for an economic laissez-faire philosophy. It is believed that what is true for biological organisms has to be true for economic organisms as well.

Thus, the concept of an "economic" human being has evolved from these intellectual traditions and has become the dogma of the American corporate world. Guided by the desirability of a competitive free market, characterizing the external environment, and an economic human being, characterizing the internal environment, organizations consider it ideal to create conditions that facilitate individual autonomy and complete freedom of choice. In addition, it is acceptable to use information to one's own advantage and to compete intensely among individuals to maximize personal benefits. These conditions simply preclude the possibility of altruistic behavior.

Although organizations promote selfish and egotistic (rather than unselfish and altruistic) behaviors on the basis of these dual assumptions—free competition and an economic human being, both assumptions have been found to be untrue. Economists such as Galbraith (1967), for instance, suggest that American corporations do not operate in an ideal free market environment. Markets do not control the corporations; rather, the corporations control the markets and consequently are able to engage in monopoly pricing, price cutting to eliminate competition, employment and customer discrimination, deceptive advertising, environmental pollution, and so on. All these forms of egotistic behavior at the organizational level directly produce many social "evils" rather than social "goods." They have led to public criticism of business ethics and a public demand for corporate altruism and social responsibility.

The "economic" human being assumption has also been challenged by psychologists (Maslow, 1965; McGregor, 1960; Schein, 1980). Contemporary motivation theories suggest that human nature is not limited simply to maximizing personal economic benefits. It is much more complex. It includes both social and self-actualizing tendencies, as Schein's "complex" human being concept would suggest. Thus, organizational practices that promote individual competition and maximize personal benefits may not be in tune with human nature as we know it today.

In addition to the influence of the economic assumptions of a free market and the economic human being, the development of a self-centered psychology in America operates against giving altruism its rightful place in organizational contexts. America has promoted a psychology of the self that Edward Sampson (1988) describes as a "self-contained" individualism. It is a conception of the self that is based on "the belief that each of us is an entity separate from every other . . . with a sharp boundary that stops at one's skill" (Spence, 1985, p. 1288). It is exclusive of others. Altruistic behavior, on the other hand, requires a conception of self that is more inclusive of others. As a result, altruism is not perceived as important or as beneficial as it might be in other cultures. Instead, there is a strong emphasis on individual accomplishment and material prosperity, even at the expense of others.

Historically, the evolution of this self-contained individualism can be traced back to medieval Europe (Morris, 1972) and to its crystallization in the 16th century (Baumeister, 1987). Before this time, conceptions of the self were of individuals who had only limited control over their environments. External forces played a more determinate role, and the notion of an individual independent of others was quite foreign. For example, in the Greek Oedipus cycle, circumstance rather than personality was central: "The personal character of Oedipus is really irrelevant to his misfortunes, which were decreed by fate irrespective of his own desires" (Morris, 1972, p. 4). In contrast, we find an emphasis on individualism and personal control by the time of Shakespeare's tragedies in the Renaissance: "The fault, dear Brutus, is not in our stars, but in ourselves" (*Julius Caesar,* Act 1, Scene ii, line 134, quoted in Morris, 1972, p. 4). These notions of self-authorship and self-contained individualism reached their zenith or most exemplary expressions in the American culture of the 20th century. Spence (1985) argues that "individualism is so central to the American character and its positive aspects so taken for granted that it is difficult to conceive of any alternative kind of self-conception" (p. 1287).

The American emphasis on individualism arose largely from the country's early ties to the Protestant work ethic and its emphasis on individual achievement (Weber, 1958a). Protestantism brought a relatively radical view of humankind's relationship to God. There were no intermediaries such as a pope. Instead, a direct relationship existed between God and the individual. As a result, individuals were directly responsible to their Maker. The glorification of God became the principal aim of one's life and could only be accomplished through productive work. Work was perceived as humankind's calling, and not to work would be to risk falling from grace:

> To lose time, through sociability, "idle talk," extravagance, even through taking more sleep than is necessary for health (6 to at most 8 hours), is considered worthy of total moral condemnation. Franklin's remark that "time is money" is not yet found, but the proposition is true, so to speak, in a spiritual sense: it is infinitely valuable, since every hour lost is taken away from work in the service of God's glory, hence passive contemplation is also valueless, indeed in some cases actually objectionable. (Weber, in Runciman, 1978, pp. 141-142)

In this system, the attainment of worldly success through hard work was interpreted as a sign of God's grace. And although strict adherence to this philosophy was perhaps limited in reality, the moral imperatives of working hard, making a success of oneself, and becoming materially prosperous survived (Spence, 1985, p. 1289). Over time, these beliefs became secularized and incorporated into a national value system. In addition, they combined with a belief that success depended on a measure of individual competition. It was not enough to work hard; the real measure and sign of achievement was to "win" in the competition against others. Individualism and with it the notion of personal rights and freedom became sacred values. These beliefs and those of the philosophy of the Enlightenment ultimately guided the formulation of the Declaration of Independence and the Constitution. As such, both documents spell out the assumption that the individual is supreme and that government exists to serve the individual and not the other way around: "We hold these truths to be self-evident, that all men are created equal, that they are endowed by their creator with certain inalienable rights." These ideals derive directly from a notion of individualism where freedom is based on personal or individual expression.

These beliefs are so ingrained in our sense of self that children, at an early age, are expected to learn self-reliance and independence (Spence, 1985). For example, parents—especially the fathers of boys—encourage their children to be competitive and to win and to be the best (Block, 1973). Spence also notes that in our theories of ego and moral development, the highest stage is one in which the individual reaches an autonomous level above the acceptance of and the conformity to standards of society (e.g., Kohlberg, 1969; Loevinger, 1976). Such a value system fosters an individualism that is narrowly defined in terms of self-interest. It precludes a sense of self that might be more inclusive—one that would recognize interdependence and a sense of community. At best, it encourages only limited acts of altruism—the utilitarian mode—those that also serve the interests of the actor.

◩ WHY IS ALTRUISM NEEDED IN ORGANIZATIONS?

As Nobel laureate Herbert Simon (1990) observed: "It is of no little moment for the human future whether people are necessarily and consistently selfish, as is sometimes argued in population genetics and economics, or whether there is a significant place for altruism in the scheme of human behavior" (p. 1665). The fact is that there are distinct liabilities to a worldview that emphasizes individualism to the exclusion of responsibility to a larger public good. Of course, it cannot be denied that emphasis on individual accomplishment and the notion that time is money have created a fast-paced competitive climate that has brought technological advancement and great material prosperity to Western countries. But it cannot also be equally denied that such progress has not been without a rather heavy price. Examples abound of the unhealthy search for self-interest, as cited in the first chapter. Even the academic community is not immune from this sense of unconcerned individual gain. In a panel discussion on the topic of growing scientific fraud, Robert Petersdorf, dean of the medical school at the University of California at San Diego, observed that science is too competitive and entrepreneurial, with an emphasis on winning. He argued that measuring achievement on the quantity of an individual's publications and research grants has led to greater fraud (Spence, 1985).

Furthermore, this sense of individualism might well explain the rise of the "me generation"—a people trapped in narcissistic self-absorption. In the wake of material prosperity has come a decreased dependence on others, as services, formerly provided by the family or community, are now purchased from the "care-provider" businesses. Technological advances and geographically dispersed career opportunities have contributed to a more mobile society, which has meant a growing sense of aloneness and alienation. These trends and developments, and their effects, are a powerful but sad commentary on the price of egotism that stems from an undue emphasis on the almost unrestrained exercise of individual autonomy and freedom.

What is needed is a greater sense of balance between this individualism and a concern for the larger community. In his book *The Duality of Human Existence,* David Bakan (1966) proposed that each of us has two fundamental but opposed senses: a sense of self that is demonstrated in self-protectiveness and self-assertiveness, and a sense of selflessness that manifests itself in communion with others. Although both are necessary for survival, the difficulty facing individuals and societies is to reconcile these two polar senses. Dawes (1975) characterizes this difficulty as the "commons dilemma," borrowing the concept from Hardin (1968). In the West, the balance is tilted in favor of self-assertiveness; in the East, in favor of communion. There is a need to move more toward a point of balance—to cultivate a concern for the larger community rather than an indifference to it. For example, Deutsch's (1973) work on competition and cooperation demonstrated the positive achievements of co-operative groups in which members sought to help an entire group in reaching its goals. Recent research on Japanese and European manufacturing strategies, where collective achievements are rewarded over individual goals, further supports the notion that a more inclusive self can lead to greater effectiveness (e.g., Ouchi, 1981; Schein, 1980).

In addition, studies in psychology have shown that striving for individual achievement can often be self-defeating and counterproductive. Spence and Helmreich (1983) found that interpersonally competitive individuals were less likely to achieve than peers who were less competitive. The compulsively driven Type-A individuals may succeed in the short run only at the expense of their long-term health (Jenkins, Rosenman, & Zyzanski, 1974). The phenomenal economic success of Japan and Asian countries is testimony to the role that a more inclusive self, a more altruistically driven self, can play in increasing rather than decreasing business effectiveness. The rewards of altruism may stretch significantly beyond "good business sense" to our own personal health and well-being. In a controversial study, Harvard psychologist David McClelland (1995; McClelland & Burnham, 1995) found a surprising link between altruism and the body's immune system. He showed students a film of Mother Teresa working among the poor and sick of India. Afterward, tests showed increased levels of immunoglobulin A, an antibody used by the body against respiratory infections. Even students who expressed a dislike for Mother Teresa showed the enhanced immune response (Growald & Luks, 1988). Perhaps the benefits of altruism may be far greater than we realize.

Business organizations in America are in a transition (Salk, 1973), moving from an industrial to a postindustrial stage. The industrial era promoted organizational philosophies of self-centered, competitive relations within the framework of a mechanistic and bureaucratic structure. It also promoted cultural norms and values of personal achievement and independence. The contemporary postindustrial environment, however, is different; it is more complex and turbulent. To respond to such an environment, organizations can no longer be viewed merely as economic machines designed for technological progress and for the personal benefit of those who control them. Instead, they must be seen as sociotechnical systems responsive to human needs both in their external and internal environments. As human systems, organizations must develop the moral obligation to respond to the needs of consumers, minority groups, and others in their external environments. In other words, organizational structures and philosophies need to shift toward more organic forms with collaborative relations and a sense of purpose that includes the organization's effectiveness as well as the improvement of the quality of life of its members. The individuals' personal values also need to shift from self-centered achievement and independence to altruistic self-actualization and interdependence.

These value shifts are also evident in debates on technology versus humanism. Scholars argue, much more than ever before, in favor of limiting technological and economic benefits when these are achieved at the expense of human values (Braden, 1970; Reich, 1971). As Mintzberg (1982b) points out, "economic morality" cannot be promoted if it amounts to "social immorality." Such trends in the thinking of management scholars clearly attest to the need for promoting altruism in organizations.

◎ THE SOURCES OF SPIRITUAL STRENGTH

The preceding discussion reviewed the formidable obstacles to the very idea of moral altruism, and much more so to its practice in the business organization. It also pointed out that the need for altruism and altruistic behaviors is equally great. For the charismatic leader, it is, unquestionably, an ethical imperative. How, then, can charismatic leaders prepare themselves and their organizations to meet the challenging demands of their role? As discussed in Chapter 4, charismatic leadership is essentially transformational in nature— that is, the self-transformation of the leader and of the followers. The strength and resources needed for this purpose go well beyond the mere material domain; leaders need to draw on their inner spiritual strength, on their spirituality. The sections that follow explore the nature of spirituality and its manifestation in the cognitive, affective, and moral character of the individual; the nature of charismatic leadership in the context of the spiritual experiences of both the leader and followers when its practice is consistent with moral principles. The chapter concludes with some observations on the sources that the spiritual sages of all time recommend that leaders can draw on for the spiritual strength, solace, and inspiration they need to exercise the leadership that is uplifting both to themselves and to their followers.

Spirituality: Its Nature and Manifestations

The *Concise Oxford English Dictionary* (1964) defines *spiritual* as "of spirit as opp[osed] to matter; of the soul esp[ecially] as acted on by God; . . . inner nature of man" (p. 1236). It defines *spirit* as the "intelligent or immaterial part of man, soul" (p. 1236). These meanings suggest the dual nature—material and spiritual—of human beings. However, it was clearly recognized as far back as Aristotle that the union between spirit (soul) and matter is so perfect that only one being is present. Just as a piece of pottery is not clay plus the shape in which it is formed, but shaped clay, in the same manner philosophical tradition that goes back to Aristotle and Aquinas has always regarded a human being not as a body plus a spirit (soul), but as matter made real by a spirit (soul), resulting in a unique person.

The human being as a whole person functions through the use of the intellect and the will. The intellect uses the external sensory inputs (sight, hearing, touch, taste, smell) and internal mental processes (memory and imagination) to penetrate into those deep levels of reality that the physical senses and processes cannot access; it does so through abstract concepts and ideas that help to make sense of and give meaning to things, events, and people that one observes and experiences, and with which one interacts. The will is the power that acts in light of intellectual knowledge. Although the cognitive and volitional behaviors occur in the spiritual domain, they are, nevertheless, influenced—that is, facilitated or hampered—by the material nature of human beings. For example, rhetoric can be used to arouse the imagination that can either elucidate or detract from rational arguments. Likewise, the hedonistic inclinations of our material being influence our emotions, which can, in turn, make it easy or difficult for us to act as our intellect directs. The faculties of intellect and will that are unique to human beings enable us to ascend from the domain of sense experience to the domain of thought—to a higher reality, which Plato termed the "eternal" unchanging objects of thought—that is, ideas (Adler, 1981).

Assuming the existence of an ideational domain in human life, how do we describe the concept of spirituality and its place in that domain? If we search for its meaning in the various religions of the world, spirituality is a concept that is difficult to define in a manner that is universally acceptable. Because the contents of religious beliefs and rites differ widely from age to age and from one society to another, it might be difficult to arrive at a consensus on what constitutes spirituality. However, if we analyze the spiritual experience per se and its behavioral manifestations among individuals of different religious persuasion instead of looking into specific religious beliefs and rites, it becomes self-evident that there is much accord on the understanding and appreciation of the essence of spirit at three levels: cognitive, affective, and manifest behavior. The commonality of the spiritual experience at each of the three levels transcends the diversity of religious practices and beliefs. Like material objects, spirituality is also experienced, comprehended, felt, and acted on. It is the experience of reality at a deeper level, or at a higher level of abstraction. It is experiencing the incorporeal, or the symbolic reality underlying the mundane phenomena.

The Cognitive and Affective Levels of Spiritual Experience

At a cognitive level, spiritual experience represents a realization that, at the core of human existence, there is a set of cardinal virtues and capital vices and that the goal of human life is to live these values and overcome the vices. Unlike the technical jargon usual in the sciences, the virtues are expressed in words that are frequently used in ordinary conversation, thereby confirming that these ideas "constitute the vocabulary of everyone's thought" (Adler, 1981, p. 3). In moral theology, the human moral virtues, as different from the theological virtues of faith, hope, and charity, have been traditionally identified as prudence, justice, temperance, and fortitude. These are termed the *cardinal virtues* because around them hinge numerous human virtues or good practices that acquire moral significance when performed to facilitate the practice of the cardinal virtues. Fullinwider (1986) categorized virtues into four groups:

> (1) the moral virtues—honesty, truthfulness, decency, courage, justice; (2) the intellectual virtues—thoughtfulness, strength of mind, curiosity; (3) the communal virtues—neighbourliness, charity, self-support, helpfulness, co-operativeness, respect for others; (4) the political virtues—commitment to the common good, respect for law, responsible participation. (p. 6)

At an affective level, the spiritual experience represents complete trust and dependence on such virtues that represent a set of human values or an agent who embodies these values. In its most sublime manifestation, spiritual experience represents a complete identification with the values (or the agent) with a view to achieve an enduring blissful state of existence. The Hindu religious tradition, as expressed in the Vedas, describes this state as *sat-chit-anand;* the Christian religious tradition refers to it as attaining the "beatific vision." Phenomenologically, spiritual experience represents a cognitive and affective sense of inner being, an inner experiential ego state or a kind of consciousness that is different from the day-to-day experiences of the self in relation to its material nature or to the material world.

Thus, there is nothing mythical or unreal about spiritual experiences. On the contrary, such experiences are real. They are psychologically mediated in the sense that individuals experience spirituality when they identify with or are committed to a set of values or to an agent symbolizing these values. In Maslow's (1967) theory of metamotivation, the spiritual experiences of pursuing values such as truth, goodness, and beauty are regarded as a major part of one's self-actualization. In terms of the need-theoretic approach, spiritual experience results from the satisfaction of cognitive needs by discovering truth, altruistic needs by doing good to others, and aesthetic needs by appreciating beauty in nature or in human works of art. In Hinduism, spiritual experience implies the realization of *satyam,* truth; *sivam,* goodness; and *sundaram,* beauty (Radhakrishnan, 1962).

When we think of truth, goodness, and beauty, we are thinking about the world in which we live, "about the knowledge we have of it, the desires it arouses in us, and the admiration it elicits from us" (Adler, 1981, p. 24). In addition to need satisfaction, the values underlying truth, goodness, and beauty are so transcendent and universal that these ideas also become the touchstone by which we judge our manifest behaviors, discussed in the next section.

Spiritual Experience at the Level of Manifest Behavior

How is the spiritual experience expressed in one's manifest behavior? What are the sources of the norms, principles, and standards of human behavior in the spiritual domain? Responses to these questions generally come from the prescriptions of moral science or ethics. In Chapter 3, we discussed the nature and conditions of a morally good act. We now explore how a morally good act is necessarily an expression of a spiritual act and an indispensable condition of a truly spiritual experience.

The ability to distinguish between morally good and evil acts is critical to the formation of character that enables the individual to behave consistently in moral ways, and reveals to the observer the individual's visible moral identity. However, the knowledge of ethical principles alone (as criteria for distinguishing between good and evil acts) is futile unless the individual makes the effort to habitually incorporate these principles in his or her behavior. "It was Aristotle's position that before moral argument can be effective the soul of the listener must first have been conditioned by habits of the right kind of likes and dislikes" (Watson, 1991, p. xiii). As Walton (1988) observed: "Character is more than what simply happens to people. It is what they do to themselves" (p. 175). It constitutes an inner-directed and habitual strength of mind and will.

The acquisition of such habitual strength, also known as "the practice of virtue," is greatly facilitated by the individual's moral mentors who guide both by precept and example. Because practice makes perfect, it is imperative, in character formation, that much thought and care is given to what one practices. Because the values underlying the cardinal virtues, referred to earlier, are universally accepted, we shall briefly discuss each cardinal virtue in the context of its importance to moral behavior.

Prudence. This virtue is practiced when the individual habitually assesses, in light of right standards, the situation or issue on which a decision is required. The assessment also includes the likely favorable and unfavorable consequences of the decision for oneself as well as for others. As a result of such assessment, the individual decides to make or refrain from making the decision. The prudent person will not abdicate his or her responsibility for unethical behavior by subordinates through messages such as: Do whatever you have to do, just don't tell me about it. In addition to the relevant knowledge and expertise that must be brought to bear on the assessment, the prudent person will not only not resent that others disagree with his or her views but will actively seek such information to better assess the situation. In other words, prudence means the objective assessment of the situation and the exercise of sound judgment.

Justice. The virtue of justice requires the individual to strive constantly to give others what is their due. The "due" is interpreted to mean more than the legalistic concept of the contractual rights of others. It includes whatever others might need to fulfill their duties and exercise their rights as persons, that is, the right to life, to cultural and moral goods, material goods, and so on. In the organizational context, it means the exercise of a sense of responsibility that balances, in a fair manner, the rights of all the stakeholders—customers, employees, suppliers, government, community—as well as of the owners.

Fortitude. It is the courage to take great risks for an ideal that is worthwhile. A courageous person faces difficult situations and strives to act positively to overcome obstacles to do what is good and noble. One of the underlying characteristics of fortitude is perseverance and endurance against great odds. As Leavitt (1986) observed: "Determined people try to make it happen because they believe in it, not because the odds are on their side" (p. 95).

Temperance. The practice of this virtue involves distinguishing between what is reasonable and necessary and what is self-indulgent. Although it includes the reasonable use and satisfaction of one's sense appetites, it also involves the efficient and effective allocation of one's time, effort, and resources. Stated differently, temperance means the exercise of self-control that, in general, would lead one to avoid and resist the temptation to overindulge in hedonistic behaviors.

The practice of virtues, however these are classified, reflects the individual's struggle with two fundamental, but diametrically opposed, choices that constantly confront the individual in every context of his or her life. These choices are (a) Should my thoughts and actions be for my benefit at the cost of others? or (b) Should my thoughts and actions be for the benefit of others at my cost? The values inherent in the choice of "other before self" are universal and form part of the heritage of all cultures. This point was illustrated in Chapter 3 with examples from two religious cultures, Catholic and Hindu, that have fundamentally different approaches to the sources of religious truth that illumine the path to moral behavior. In the context of the charismatic leadership phenomenon, the transformational role adopted by the charismatic leader requires a principal concern for the benefit of others even when such concern involves considerable cost to the leader. This is so because the leader's personal sacrifices become the authentic, visible signs of commitment and dedication to his or her ideal vision, which is one of the critical factors that moves the followers to attribute charisma to the leader.

To recapitulate the discussion so far: Spiritual experience is not an aberration. It is of the very essence of human beings to function in the spiritual domain. To so function, the individual's behavior tends to be governed by the habitual practice of virtues. In the final analysis, it is the spiritual experience that enables each person to grow and fully realize the tremendous potential that is unique to that person.

> Of all living creatures, only humans have the power to shape their own character, to choose between honourable and dishonourable behavior, to tell the truth or deceive, to exploit or respect others, to work hard or slack off. Each decision so shapes the person that subsequent behavior is more predictable. (Walton, 1988, p. 176)

If a good moral character is of the essence of every human being, then with much greater reason does it become so of charismatic leaders who by their "vision, values, and determination add soul to the organization" (Leavitt, 1986, pp. 222-223).

Charismatic Leadership: Its Spiritual Dimensions

As discussed previously, the charismatic leadership phenomenon is characterized by the following features. First, it is a relational phenomenon whose existence depends primarily on the followers' experience of dependence on the leader as an influencing agent. Second, in this relationship, followers develop a strong emotional bond with the leader, characterized by an abiding faith and an unwavering trust. Third, very often the development of such an emotional bond with the leader is triggered by the followers' experience of some contextual crises that have affected them personally. Finally, charismatic leadership comes into being when the followers perceive and attribute certain characteristics to the leader such as the embodiment of idealized vision, extraordinary abilities, and unconventional behavioral manifestations.

These characteristics of the charismatic leadership phenomenon are also echoed in our spiritual experiences. In almost all religions, spirituality is associated with a belief in relating oneself with a higher-order influencing agent. The relationship is one of dependence on this superhuman/supernatural agent manifested in different forms in different religions. For some, the agent is perceived to be another human, a guru—the supreme teacher—or a saint, who embodies to a high degree of perfection all the good and noble qualities to which human beings can aspire. Some even perceive the physical manifestations of nature itself to be so overpowering that they develop a dependence on it with awe and wonder. For others, the agent is conceived as an abstraction in the form of God, the supreme being—omniscient, omnipotent, and omnipresent; in some religions, such an agent is an impersonal being, in others, a personal being.

In this dependent spiritual relationship, followers of various religions also experience a strong emotional bond with the agent and demonstrate unconditional trust and unquestioning faith in the agent to guide their behavior. Regardless of the form in which the agent is perceived, the followers attribute extraordinary idealized and visionary qualities to the agent. Furthermore, while relating to an idealized agent, it is not uncommon that the spiritual experiences of dependence, trust, faith, and so on among the followers of various religions might also be triggered by the experiences of crisis in their life.

Although there is this surface resemblance, in the religious contexts, between our experiences of charismatic leadership and spirituality, such resemblance does not necessarily imply that the leadership phenomenon has a spiritual dimension to it. To demonstrate the spiritual dimensions of the charismatic leadership phenomenon, one has to consider the psychological nature of our experiences of both the leadership and the spirituality phenomena and uncover the relationship at a much deeper level. For this purpose, we need to consider the different components of the leadership phenomenon, each of which contains a spiritual dimension. These components are the spirituality in leadership experience, the rituals that reinforce the leader's influence, the self-identity of the leader, and the leader's exercise of power and the use of empowering practices. Our focus here is on the spirituality in leadership experience, the leader's exercise of power, and the use of empowering practices.

Spirituality in Leadership Experience

In the history of humankind, religious leaders and social reformers have continually experimented with new forms of values and ideals to improve the existing conditions. In the organizational context, the leadership role has been viewed as the role of managing meanings because organizations are systems of shared meanings (Pfeffer 1981; Smith & Peterson, 1988). Charismatic leaders provide meaning to an organization's goals, ideologies, and values and strive to achieve them by establishing a new order that replaces the old one. One central religious belief in Hinduism, as stated in the Bhagavad Gita, asserts that when from time to time, the world gets engulfed in vice through the acts of evil agents, God takes human form to eliminate vice and vindicate virtue and the virtuous, thereby establishing peace and order for humankind. Such beliefs reinforce the idea that in the eyes of the followers, the charismatic leaders who are committed to achieve their professed idealized vision are like a God figure. The followers tend to identify with their leaders and internalize the ideals and values professed by the leaders. The psychological outcomes of the self-growth-oriented identification and internalization processes represent the spiritual experiences of the follower, at both the cognitive and emotional levels.

For the leaders, on the other hand, the formulation of an idealized set of values that constitutes the vision—that is, the meaning they create for the organization and their commitment to the realization of this vision—represents the spiritual experience. Most religious leaders develop their vision of the perfect, the idealized, and eternal dharma or righteousness after being exposed to the limitations, imperfections, sorrows, and suffering of the finite environment—as in the case of Buddha or Francis of Assisi. Reflections on the experiences of the imperfect material world give rise to the spiritual experience of the perfect, idealized representation of the world.

Charismatic leaders in a nonreligious context go through a similar process: from experiencing the limitations of the status quo to the experiencing of an idealized state or a vision for the future that is discrepant from the status quo.

The cognitive realization of an idealized vision is a profoundly transforming spiritual experience. The essence of the experience is that transformational or charismatic leaders identify with or personally relate to a set of values that raise them to "higher levels of motivation and morality" (Burns, 1978, p. 20). The leader's commitment to higher levels of morality and his or her self-actualizing motivation to achieve the vision is often manifested in the leader's fortitude or in the form of taking personal risks and making personal sacrifices. Although personal risks and sacrifices by themselves do not necessarily indicate spiritual experience, what is noteworthy is that the transforming spiritual experience resulting from the leader's commitment to the idealized vision becomes a powerful motivational force to bear and, even gladly, suffer the hardships and sacrifices that may be necessary.

Spirituality and Power

Charismatic leaders are known to engage in socialized rather than personalized power. Socialized power is expressed in self-controlled and altruistic ways for the service of others, whereas personalized power is expressed in impulsive, aggressive, and self-aggrandized ways for one's own benefit (McClelland, 1985). The exercise of socialized power by the leader thus implies that the leader practices the cardinal virtues and takes personal risks and makes personal sacrifices for the benefit of the followers. The need to exercise socialized power forms a significant part of the spiritual self of the moral person. On the other hand, the effort to gain material wealth and status through personalized power and the hedonistic attachment to such outcomes is the product of eros or kama in the competitive, self-centered, individualized self, and not of the spiritual self.

The path to the realization of the spiritual self, as prescribed in the Eight Beatitudes of the Sermon on the Mount (Matthew 5-7) or in other religious scriptures, essentially involves that the individual acts simultaneously on two fronts. The individual regards the mundane world as transitory or illusory—maya in the Hindu tradition—and, therefore, develops an emotional detachment from it. At the same time, the individual develops a bonding with the spiritual reality, which alone has permanence, is unchanging, and endures. Emotional detachment allows the leader to develop prudence and the proper perspective of the purpose and role of people, things, and events. The bonding with the spiritual reality that results from the leader's commitment to the higher purpose and the emotional detachment from the mundane reality enables the leader to overcome personal vices and to cope with sorrows and sufferings.

Furthermore, the leader views these events as a rich source of inner strength and insights of the human condition, which are essential if the leader is to adopt the needed compassion for and understanding of his or her followers. As Roland (1988) puts it, "As the person becomes increasingly involved in the realization of the spiritual self, he or she still relates to others and fulfills responsibilities, but without the intense looking to the other for the fulfillment of wishes, esteem and the desire to be needed" (p. 307). In other words, the need for socialized power and the manifest behaviors to fulfill such needs on the part of the charismatic leaders through personal sacrifices are the reflections of their increased involvement in the spiritual self and their detachment from the individualized self.

Spirituality and Empowerment

As discussed at length in Chapter 4, the nature of the influence of charismatic leaders on the followers is characterized as transformational rather than transactional. The followers achieve self-transformation not through transactions in social exchange of valued resources but through the emotional bonding, identification with the leader, and internalization of the idealized vision advocated by the leader. The primary objective of bringing about the self-transformation in the followers is to enable them to achieve an inner strength or a set of cognitive beliefs regarding their capability to pursue and be involved in the realization of the vision.

In influencing the followers to achieve the inner strength and capability, the actions of charismatic leaders are designed to empower the followers. The experience of being empowered by an influencing agent who is strong and virtuous, trustworthy, supportive, and nurturing is a spiritual experience. The followers' dependence on such an agent does not imply a mindless, servile, or parasitic subordination. Rather, it implies a dependence that is of the nature of a growth-oriented identification with the leader. This allows followers to draw inspiration from the leader so that they might be self-efficacious and, like the leader, achieve a similar self-transformation. Charismatic leaders do not force followers to be dependent on them. Therefore, the followers' dependence does not result from fear of rejection or other forms of threats. Instead, charismatic leaders lead by personal examples of virtuous acts and by the idealized content of the vision, the attraction of which is greatly enhanced by the inspirational manner in which it is articulated. The followers are, thus, inspired to follow the leader's example, and they do so with complete autonomy and of their own volition. They choose to be dependent on the leader because they are convinced that the path they follow will eventually lead to the realization of their own deepest hopes and aspirations.

The nature of this dependence is similar to that of a serious student who trustingly follows the guidance and direction of the teacher in order to grow and develop into an independent exponent of the subject matter. Such dependence is best exemplified by the *chela*-guru (student-teacher) relationship in Hindu asceticism. In this relationship, the guru is revered and almost worshipped as a godhead. Through this reverence and worship, the students seek the guru's blessings so that they might attain the level of knowledge, wisdom, and spiritual development of the guru. In fact, a prayer commonly used by students to obtain such blessings is, "Oh Lord, through your grace the mute speaks and the lame conquers the mountain. I pray thee for your grace." The prayer obviously has a spiritual connotation; the student seeks to be empowered. The empowering experience that underlies this relationship has a strong spiritual element that substantially affects and forms the student's spiritual life. In much the same way, the follower depends on a charismatic leader for self-transformation.

In conclusion, although leadership can take various forms, such as task-oriented, people-oriented, participative, and charismatic or transformational leadership, it is only when leadership takes the charismatic form that the spiritual dimension comes much more to the fore. In the task, people, and participative leadership roles, the leader neither pursues any idealized vision nor attempts any growth-oriented self-transformation. The self-identity of such leaders can be characterized in terms of an emphasis on either individualized "I-ness" self (task-oriented leadership role) or familial we-self (people-oriented and participative leadership roles). But one can notice the presence of the spiritual self when true leadership is exercised—that is, when the leader brings about change in the status quo through the growth-oriented self-transformation of the leader and of the followers.

At the cognitive level, the spiritual dimension of the self is expressed in the sense of the profound consciousness of the eternal values of truth, beauty, and goodness represented by the vision of the leader. At the affective level, spirituality is manifested in the emotional bonding with and trust and faith in these values. At the manifest behavior level, spirituality radiates primarily through the leader's virtuous life that places the interest and concerns of others before those of one's self, despite the personal risks and sacrifices that may be and, in fact, are inevitably involved.

The Development of the Leader as a Moral Person

As discussed previously, charismatic leadership is essentially transformational in nature—that is, self-transformation of the leader and of the followers. Charismatic leaders readily recognize that the self-transformation ought to begin with one's self. In the context of ethical management, Blanchard and Peale (1988) offer inspiring and practical principles of ethical power: purpose, pride, patience, persistence, and perspective. We briefly discuss these principles because charismatic leaders too can tap these sources of ethical power as they go about their task of self-transformation.

Purpose

The critical set of behaviors of the charismatic leader is to evaluate the status quo; to formulate and articulate a vision that is discrepant from the status quo; and to take the means—personal sacrifice, building trust among followers, and using unconventional behavior—to achieve the vision (Conger & Kanungo, 1987). The charismatic leader often exercises his or her ethical power by subjecting the vision as well as the means to achieve it to the rigorous scrutiny of the purpose that it is intended to serve. What higher purpose does the vision serve? In the context of the business organization, it is universally admitted that the business must be profitable. Influential business magazines, such as *Forbes* and *Fortune,* and business textbooks blatantly suggest that the purpose of business is "to maximize profits and to maximize the wealth of those who own the business organization. It is a commentary on society that these attitudes and expectations largely go unexamined and unchallenged" (Watson, 1991, p. 34). But the ethical leader stops to ask: Are profits a means or an end in itself? Corporations committed to a higher purpose "exist to provide society with the goods and services it needs, to provide employment, and to create a surplus of wealth [profit] with which to improve the general standard of living and quality of life" (O'Toole, 1985, p. 49).

The scrutiny of the vision in the perspective of its higher purpose will cause the leader to practice primarily the virtues of prudence and justice. Furthermore, the habit of questioning the purpose of one's actions in light of ethical principles demonstrates the strength of the leader's character that enhances the followers' perception of the trustworthiness of the leader.

Pride

The charismatic leader obviously needs to have high self-esteem. This self-esteem originates from a healthy pride in one's accomplishments as well as the esteem of one's followers. However, the leader's behaviors are not designed merely to gain the acceptance of the followers. For example, in formulating the vision the leader ought to take into account the needs and aspirations of the followers, but the leader ought not to allow the desire to be accepted by the followers to compromise the vision when such compromise will jeopardize the higher purpose. In other words, the leader does not look to the followers for affiliative assurance (Boyatzis, 1984) to reinforce his or her self-love but rather for transforming the followers to accept and realize the vision.

The charismatic leader needs to exercise power over his or her followers but the origin of this power is the leader's identification with the objectives derived from the higher purpose. Consequently, in the exercise of such power the leader is seen as a helpful coach and mentor rather than a tyrannical dictator. As Donald Hall of Hallmark observed: "Being able to manage people is not standing over them with a whip but being able to understand people who work for them and around them and maximizing people's potential" (quoted in Watson, 1991, pp. 289-290). Charismatic leaders exhibit healthy pride not vanity. The dividing line between healthy pride and vanity is unbelievably thin because of the strong egoistic tendency in human beings, but charismatic leaders recognize that inordinate self-love is a human vice and not a virtue.

Patience

As the charismatic leader works toward the realization of the vision, he or she is certain to come across obstacles from the environment (internal or external) or from the reluctance of the followers to accept and be committed to the vision. The reasons for the latter might be lack of understanding of the vision and its positive features or simply a lack of trust in the leader. It takes time and effort to overcome such obstacles that are inevitable in a worthy and noble endeavor, hence, the need for patience. A patient person bears the present difficulties with calm and serenity because of his or her faith in the vision.

There are two aspects to this faith. The first aspect is the leader's strong belief in the truth and value of the higher purpose and in his or her vision of the future as the best way to serve that higher purpose. The second aspect relates to the strength of the leader's conviction in spiritual beliefs. When a leader believes in a higher purpose or a being representing the higher purpose (for some, that Being is God), the leader develops an inner realization that, in good time, the difficulties will be resolved. The faith referred to here is not fatalism that inevitably paralyzes action. Rather, both aspects of faith—the vision and the spiritual convictions—contribute to the leader's constancy of purpose that leads him or her to continue undaunted with what needs to be done in the unshaken belief that the present difficulties are part of the progress toward realizing the vision. This will particularly be the case with a leader who strives to exercise prudence and fortitude. As discussed in the first section, the practice of prudence enables one to properly assess all facts and circumstances surrounding one's decisions, and the practice of fortitude develops the capacity to act positively in the midst of difficulties. The relevance of prudence for charismatic leadership is reflected in the charismatic leader's need to be sensitive to the environment; the relevance of fortitude is demonstrated by the fact that the charismatic leader is called on to perform behaviors that involve great personal risks and sacrifices. As a result, the patient leader who is in the habit of practicing prudence and fortitude will not be inclined to resort to unethical practices when things do not go as planned.

Persistence

The power of persistence is best captured in Winston Churchill's bulldog-like perseverance—that is, to never, never give up. Persistence does not mean a stubborn obstinacy. Rather, the leader will not allow difficulties to weaken his or her resolve to stay the course; instead, he or she continues to take the steps necessary, even those involving personal risk and sacrifice, to achieve the vision. It is perfectly human to justify unethical practices when one feels overwhelmed by insurmountable internal or external difficulties. The practice of fortitude allows one to strive to overcome difficulties not because it is convenient or pleasant to do so, but because one's duty requires that it be done. This idea is forcefully expressed by John Hoyt Stookey of National Distillers (now Quantum Chemical) when he declared: "One of the things . . . that we mean by ethical behavior is that we will forgo profit in order to adhere to a standard of conduct. I believe that's a message a CEO needs to convey loud and clear to an organization and I find myself doing that" (quoted in Watson, 1991, p. 186).

In a society in which both individuals and organizations are obsessed with and guided by short-term gratification, the practice of patience and persistence does become a real challenge. In his Spiritual Exercises, Ignatius of Loyola proposed that in situations when one is inclined to justify the neglect of one's duty with endless rationalizations, then the individual is advised not to debate these rationalizations, but simply to make the extra effort to do what one's duty dictates.

Perspective

"Perspective is the capacity to see what is really important in any given situation" (Blanchard & Peale, 1988, p. 69). The habit of reflection is critical to acquiring a sense of perspective. And reflection is simply not possible unless one devotes some time each day to silence—a resource that has been recommended by wise men of all time and from all cultures, and yet the one resource that remains most untapped.

> If I were a doctor and I could prescribe just one remedy for all the ills of the modern world, I would prescribe silence. For even if the word of God were proclaimed in the modern world, no one would hear it, because of the panoply of noise. Therefore, *create silence.* (Kierkegaard, cited by Kreeft, 1990, p. 168)

Silence is more than refraining from noise; it is the inner silence that allows one to reflect on the higher purpose, to question one's decisions in light of that purpose, and to seek strength not to betray it. It allows one to listen to the inner stirrings of the spirit and is needed to make distinctions, between right and wrong, to discern what one ought to do.

> I am continually amazed at how clear my thinking becomes afterward, particularly if I'm faced with a big problem. It's as if the answer I am seeking exists somewhere already, just waiting for me to tune in to it. The solitude, quiet, and reflection are the tuning-in process. (Blanchard & Peale, 1988, p. 76)

The preceding discussion has touched on several suggestions available to charismatic leaders in their efforts to develop the inner strength they need to function as ethical, moral persons. The ascetical literature, however, emphasizes that the enduring effectiveness of these suggestions very much depends on their habitual practice and, more important, on a specific time the leader sets aside for the ascetical practice of "examination of conscience." No one will deny that individuals do not suddenly find themselves engaging in grave and serious unethical practices. On the contrary, examples abound that these are preceded by minor unethical lapses, which one rationalizes as being inconsequential or doing so because "everyone is doing it." The periodic examination of conscience prevents a person from, or at least alerts a person to the fact that he or she might be, treading the slippery slope of unethical behavior.

The Development of a Moral Environment

"To model love. I am the *soul* of this company. It is through me that our organization's values pass" (quoted in Blanchard & Peale, 1988, p. 89). This was the response of the chairman of Matushita Electric when asked about his primary job. The statements of the vision, mission, and policies—however numerous, well-crafted, and articulated—are futile if the leader's actions and behavior are inconsistent with these statements. Actions speak louder than words; what the leader does and values sets the ethical tone and creates the moral environment of the organization. In the 1988 Touche Ross survey of key business leaders, deans of business schools, and members of Congress on ethical standards and behavior, "73 percent recognize the CEO's ability to influence ethical behavior" (Kangas, 1988, p. 11).

Truly, the leader is the soul of the organization. For example, even in the relatively trivial area of employees' work attendance, the CEO's example has been found to be critical. In one organization, when the CEO regularly arrived at his office at 10:00 a.m., his executives came in at 9:45 a.m., but when his successor began work at 7:00 a.m., these same executives now came in at 8:00 a.m. or earlier (Stovall, 1988). However, there are other more telling examples: One manufacturer continued to produce a product known to cause illness and death; on the other hand, Johnson & Johnson immediately withdrew Tylenol from the market, at enormous costs, even though the product was completely safe (Lank, 1988). The actions of these CEOs sent clear, unambiguous messages about the ethical standards expected from their employees.

The higher purpose established for the organization by the charismatic leader becomes the starting point in creating the moral environment. The higher purpose and the values it represents convey to the followers what is acceptable and unacceptable behavior. However, to facilitate the employees' internalization of these values, the leader must develop specific codes of conduct for organizational members. The codes of conduct are useful and even necessary, but care needs to be taken in their development. For instance, in a survey of codes of conduct of more than 200 companies, the "most ignored item was personal character—it seemed not to matter" (Walton, 1988, p. 170). In addition to the codes of conduct, the leader should identify areas and issues that might be particularly susceptible to unethical conduct and develop internal policies and processes that specifically deal with them.

The leader should also create opportunities for employees to exchange ideas and experiences in the implementation of the code of conduct, as well as the difficulties they might likely encounter in acting ethically in certain situations, especially if ethical dilemmas are involved. Some organizations hold periodical retreats or discussion forums, which provide employees with the intellectual, emotional, and moral support necessary to maintain the high ethical standards expected of them.

Codes of conduct, related policies and procedures, and support structures are undoubtedly essential to the development of the organization's moral environment. However, in the final analysis, it is the charismatic leader's personal conduct that determines the effectiveness of codes, policies and procedures, and support structures. The moral environment cannot be created by the fiat of the leader. Just as Mother Teresa's work for the poorest of the poor is an external outpouring of her love for God, in much the same way, the organization's moral environment is a natural overflow of the charismatic leader's commitment to ethical principles and values that is expressed not only in terms of intellectual assent but also in his or her daily struggle to live by them.

Ohmann (1989) cites the example of an executive whose policies and practices flowed naturally from his beliefs and values. This executive believed that his talent and resources are gifts entrusted to his stewardship for the "maximum self-development and useful service to one's fellows in the hope that one may live a rich life and be a credit to his Creator. . . . It is against this frame of reference that the decisions of the moment easily fall into proper perspective" (Ohmann, 1989, pp. 66-67). As a result, he provided employees with opportunities to develop to the fullest of their potential. He held his employees accountable but, at the same time, coached them to performance levels that would justify the higher rewards. He viewed profits as a measure of the successful use of the potential of his employees. Instead of talking about employee communication programs, he spent most of his time in the field listening to his employees. He managed conflicts not by considerations of expediency or self-concern but by reference to what best served the organization's higher purpose. His basic values not only led to consistency in his decisions and behavior that made him dependable and trustworthy but also gave meaning and significance to even the otherwise routine and inconsequential activities of the workplace. The resulting moral environment truly reflected the soul of the organization and enabled its members to internalize its values, which became a firm and enduring foundation for their ethical behavior.

▨ CONCLUSION

The discussion in this chapter began with an exploration of two antithetical situations: the obstacles to altruistic behavior in organizations, and the need for this behavior in organizations. We considered the obstacles posed by sociohistorical forces greatly influenced by social Darwinism and hedonistic psychology. We also considered the need for organizations to move toward more organic structures and philosophies that emphasize collaborative relations and a sense of purpose that includes the needs and concerns of all its stakeholders. Because organizational leaders bear the responsibility to bring about these major transformations in beliefs, values, and behavior, their preparation for this formidable task requires that they draw on their inner spiritual strength and resources. For this purpose, the chapter examined the nature of spirituality and its manifestation in the cognitive, affective, and moral behavior or character of the individual.

It is of the very essence of human beings to function in the spiritual domain, and the commonality of the spiritual experience transcends the diversity of religious practices and beliefs. At the cognitive level, spiritual experience represents a realization that, at the core of human existence, there is a set of cardinal virtues and capital vices, and the goal of human beings is to live the virtues and overcome the vices. At the affective level, the spiritual experience represents a state of blissful existence resulting from complete trust and dependence on these values or on an agent who embodies them. At the level of manifest behavior, the spiritual experience is expressed in the individual's moral behavior resulting from a struggle with two fundamental, but diametrically opposed, choices: action for the benefit of self at the cost of others versus action for the benefit of others at the cost of self.

To uncover the relationship between the phenomena of spirituality and charismatic leadership, we explored the different components of the leadership phenomenon that contain a spiritual dimension. We saw that the spiritual self is present in the leadership role of bringing about change in the status quo to achieve an idealized vision through the self-transformation of the leader and of the followers. At the cognitive level, spirituality is expressed in the sense of the profound consciousness of the eternal values incorporated in the leader's vision. At the affective level, it is manifested in the emotional bonding with and trust and faith in these values. At the manifest behavior level, it radiates through the leader's virtuous life that places the interest of others before those of one's self, despite the costs that may be involved. In light of this discussion, it is clear that spirituality is the quintessence of charismatic leadership. It explains its underlying strength and provides the leader with the means to develop as a moral person and to create the organization's moral environment that is conducive for ethical behavior.

6

Cultural Contingencies of Leadership

The leadership phenomenon has played a dominant role, for better or for worse, in the functioning of groups, organizations, and institutions in every human society. Previous chapters have discussed the modal orientations in leadership, the ethical dimensions in leadership motivation and leadership influence processes, and some approaches to preparing for ethical leadership. This discussion, however, has been in the sociocultural context of Europe and North America. The study of leadership along cross-cultural dimensions has received little attention. For instance, we do not know what sociocultural characteristics facilitate or hinder leader effectiveness, or in what way societal cultures influence the nature of the leadership function and the leader's role behaviors (Dorfman, 1994). With increasing globalization, the knowledge of the influence of culture on leadership effectiveness has now assumed greater importance for the management of organizations in general, and multi-national corporations in particular. It is equally, if not more, important for public and private sector organizations in developing countries with emerging markets because the introduction of change and its sound management depends, to a considerable extent, on the efforts and initiatives of leaders in these organizations.

Hence, the need for this chapter. More specifically, we explore the cross-cultural studies of the trends or modalities of leadership, with a focus on the emerging modal orientation in leadership. Because the previous chapters considered leadership primarily in terms of the Western ethos, the discussion in this chapter will be developed in the context of non-Western cultures, norms, and values, in particular, those of developing countries. We examine the culture-fit of the leader role behaviors and influence processes relative to these cultures. We also examine the compatibility of the prevailing cultural norms and values with the altruistic ethic that, we have argued, is critical to effective leadership.

▧ INFLUENCE OF CULTURE ON LEADERSHIP EFFECTIVENESS

The discussion on leadership research in Chapter 2 identified four major leader roles—task, social, participative, and charismatic—and two leadership influence processes—transactional and transformational. Each leadership role serves the organization and its members in a unique manner. The task, social, and participative roles are directed at the effective supervision and maintenance of the status quo, whereas the charismatic role serves to bring about the transformation of both the members and the systems of the organization. In the task, social, and participative roles, the leader uses mostly the transactional influence process, whereas in the charismatic role, the leader uses the transformational influence process. However, when we discuss how cultural variables influence leadership effectiveness, we shall consider both the leader role and the social influence process that is characteristic of the role. For this purpose, we first propose a conceptual framework that identifies the major cultural dimensions that might facilitate or hinder leadership effectiveness in developing countries.

The earliest research efforts on organizational leadership across cultures involved simple questionnaires measuring a range of attitudes and actions of managers without creating theoretical frameworks to demonstrate how research results might be explained across cultures (e.g., Bass & Burger, 1979; Haire, Ghiselli, & Porter, 1966). Following these initial studies, several scholars have developed conceptual schemes to study organizational behavior in cross-cultural contexts (Hofstede, 1993; Kanungo & Jaeger, 1990; Triandis, 1994; Trompenaars, 1993). The most influential among these has been Hofstede (1980), who identified four cultural dimensions: individualism/collectivism, power distance, uncertainty avoidance, and masculinity/femininity. Hofstede describes these dimensions as follows:

Individualism "implies a loosely knit social framework in which people are supposed to take care of themselves and their immediate families only, whereas *collectivism* is characterized by a tight social framework in which people distinguish between in-groups and out-groups; they expect their in-groups (relatives, clan, organizations) to look after them, and in exchange for that they feel they owe absolute loyalty to it" (p. 45).

Power distance is "the extent to which a society accepts the fact that power in institutions and organizations is distributed unequally" (p. 45).

Uncertainty avoidance is "the extent to which a society feels threatened by uncertain and ambiguous situations by providing career stability, establishing more formal rules, not tolerating deviant ideas and behaviors, and believing in absolute truths and attainment of expertise" (p. 46).

Masculinity denotes "the extent to which the dominant values in society are 'masculine,' that is, assertiveness, the acquisition of money and things, and not caring for others, the quality of life, or people" (p. 46).

These dimensions have proved useful for the study of organizational behavior across cultures. Several other scholars (e.g., Earley, 1993; Erez, 1994; Triandis, 1993) have probed in depth the individualism/collectivism dimension, which appears to be the most significant dimension to explain cross-cultural behavior.

Using several cultural dimensions along with Schein's (1985) work in this area, Kanungo and Jaeger (1990) developed a conceptual framework that derives managerial assumptions about work attitudes and behavior from the sociocultural characteristics. Such a model, shown in Figure 6.1, provides a reasonably comprehensive framework to explain the internal work culture of organizations in developing countries.

It will be seen from this figure that compared to the developed countries, the sociocultural environment of developing countries is characterized by relatively high uncertainty avoidance and power distance and relatively low individualism and masculinity. These dimensions are as suggested by Hofstede (1980). The additional dimension of associative thinking, which appears in Figure 6.1 and was drawn from Glenn and Glenn (1981), was suggested by Kedia and Bhagat (1988) to be useful in understanding the cultural differences between the developed and developing countries. According to Kedia and Bhagat: "In associative cultures, people utilize associations among events that may not have much logical basis, whereas in abstractive cultures, cause-effect relationships or rational Judeo-Christian types of thinking are dominant" (p. 566). In terms of this definition, Kanungo and Jaeger (1990) posit that

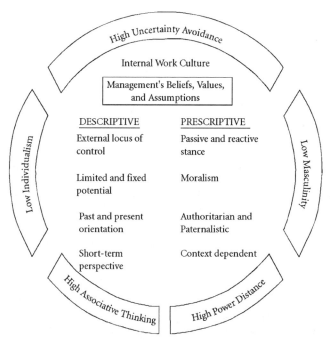

Figure 6.1. Characteristics of the Internal Work Culture of Organizations in Non-Western Societies in the Context of Their Sociocultural Environment
SOURCE: Kanungo and Jaeger (1990).

developing countries are relatively low on abstractive thinking and high on associative thinking.

The sociocultural environment determines management beliefs, values, and assumptions of workers and work behavior that characterize the organization's internal work culture. As seen in the figure, the internal work culture of developing country's organizations can be broadly categorized as (a) the descriptive assumptions about human nature and (b) the prescriptive assumptions about the guiding principles of human conduct. The descriptive assumptions relate to causality and control of outcomes, creative potential and malleability, time perspective, and time units for action. The developed and developing countries differ significantly on each of these dimensions. Thus, relative to the developed countries, managers in developing countries are more likely to assume that their employees have an external locus of control, that is, a belief that the outcomes one receives are determined by forces that are external to one's self and over which one does not have much control; have relatively fixed potential and are not easily malleable; operate from a time perspective that is past and present oriented; and have a short-term focus (Kanungo & Jaeger, 1990).

The prescriptive or normative assumptions relate to adopting a proactive or reactive stance to task performance; moral or pragmatic basis to judge success; people orientation, that is, collegial/participative or authoritarian/paternalistic; and operating from predetermined principles or according to the exigencies of the situation. In this category too there are substantial differences between the developed and developing countries. Thus, in the developing countries, managers are more likely to encourage a passive or reactive stance to task performance; judge success on moralism derived from tradition and religion; favor an authoritarian or paternalistic orientation; and accept that considerations of the context override principles and rules (Kanungo & Jaeger, 1990).

The model in Figure 6.1 provides a coherent approach to integrating the sociocultural characteristics of developing countries and the internal work culture of organizations in these countries. Its elements serve as anchors on which to ground one's exploration and understanding of the influence of cultural variables that might suggest that one leadership role is more appropriate and effective than another, and the reasons why this might be so. However, it is recognized that the implications of this model have not been fully explored in the existing literature. Although these culture dimensions and conceptual frameworks seem relevant for the study of the influence of culture on leadership roles in the context of developing countries, the specific ways in which these could be used have yet to be determined. However, initial attempts in this direction have been made (e.g., Mendonca & Kanungo, 1994). The sections that follow examine these attempts with respect to the four leadership roles previously identified.

Influence of Culture on Task and Social Leader Roles

Although the task and social roles have been explored in terms of cross-cultural research (e.g., Bond & Hwang, 1986; Sinha, 1980, 1990), perhaps the most in-depth research along these lines has been conducted by Misumi (1985) over the past 40 years in Japan. Initially triggered by contacts with Kurt Lewin, Misumi developed an extension of the Ohio State University leadership model peculiar to Japanese culture (Misumi & Peterson, 1985). He discovered that effective supervisors in Japan are those who scored high in team maintenance (consideration) and in team performance (task). The scales he used in Japan correlate very highly with the Ohio State University measures (Peterson, Maiya, & Herreid, 1987; Peterson, Smith, & Tayeb, 1987). The findings of these studies are consistent with the sociocultural context of Japan. Nevertheless, in interpreting these findings, the sociocultural characteristics of Japan were not explicitly used to explain the findings. For this reason, Misumi's findings would seem to transform what has been a contingency theory in American settings into a normative one for Japan.

In contrast to Misumi's work, Sinha (1990) explicitly used cultural variables to study the effectiveness of task and social leader roles in Indian organizations. Starting with the proposition that India has a collectivistic culture (Hofstede, 1980), the basic premise of his study is that organizational members expect personalized relationships, direction and support, and a superior-subordinate rather than a peer relationship. From this premise, he argues that a "nurturant-task" leadership would be more effective in manager-subordinate interaction in Indian organizations. The rationale for his argument is that the nurturant-task leader "cares for his subordinates, shows affection, takes personal interest in their well-being, and above all is committed to their growth" (Sinha, 1980, p. 55) but provides this nurturance only after subordinates perform the agreed job tasks.

The nurturant-task leader begins by providing clear, specific directions and performance standards supported by guidance and directions that subordinates expect. As subordinates accomplish the job tasks, they experience two critical sets of outcomes: (a) nurturant support from the manager and (b) enhanced self-confidence in meeting job goals and increased job competence. With continued success in meeting job goals, the subordinates gradually seek less direction and feel more capable of assuming responsibility. At this stage, the nurturant-task leader provides less direction and more autonomy, but continues with the nurturant approach and expectations of task performance at the agreed levels. The repeated cycle of task performance and increased autonomy exercised by subordinates is reciprocated by nurturance and reduced direction by the leader. This process results in "a relationship of understanding, warmth, and interdependence, leading to higher productivity and better growth of both the subordinates and the leader" (Sinha, 1990, p. 253).

As we can see from Figure 6.2, which depicts the nurturant-task leadership process in a developing country context, nurturant-task leadership has the potential to move the manager-subordinate relationship from a state of total

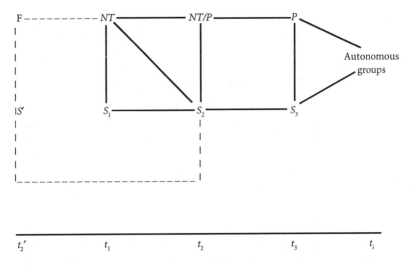

Figure 6.2. Nurturant-Task Leadership Process in a Developing Country Context

SOURCE: Sinha (1990). Reprinted by permission.
NOTE: S = subordinate; F = authoritarian; NT = nurturant-task; NT/P = combination of nurturant-task and participative; t = time point. Solid lines indicate positive nature/direction of relationship, and broken lines indicate negative nature/direction of relationship.

subordinate dependence on the manager, as in t_1, through a stage of greater autonomy for the subordinate, that is, a gradual participative approach (NT/P), as in t_2, to a fuller participative approach (P), as in t_3. The nurturant-task leadership process envisages the possibility that eventually (as in t_i), subordinates can be developed to operate as relatively autonomous groups. The model also recognizes the possibility of the manager-subordinate relationship regressing into an authoritarian mode, as in t_2'. This might occur for two reasons. One is that managers attribute the successful job accomplishments in t_1, entirely to their direction and guidance and, therefore, are apprehensive that reducing such direction would jeopardize productivity.

The other reason is that the subordinates' desire for more autonomy in t_2 might be perceived by the managers as a threat to their authority and position, which is regarded as relatively more significant in cultures characterized by high power distance. The Kanungo and Jaeger (1990) model also suggests that developing countries tend to be more collectivistic and high on power distance, which further reinforces the point that the effectiveness of task and social leadership in developing countries will be considerably enhanced by adopting

Sinha's nurturant-task leadership model. Dorfman (1994), for much the same reason, has speculated whether the nurturant-task leadership model might not also be appropriate for organizations in countries such as Mexico, Iran, and Korea, whose cultures are also collectivistic, high on power distance, and value hierarchical and personalized relationships.

Influence of Culture on the Participative Leader Role

The rationale underlying participative leadership stemmed primarily from the sociologists' approach to reduce employee alienation or a sense of power-lessness that employees were believed to experience when conditions in the workplace neither allow workers to exercise freedom and control nor provide them with the opportunity to use their potential (Blauner, 1964; Shepard, 1971). Psychologists (Kanungo, 1982; Sashkin, 1984) have also found employ-ees to become alienated if a work situation constantly frustrates an individual's need for autonomy and control. The problem with participative leadership develops when it is used as a technique to "share power" on the assumption that all employees seek and want power and its corresponding responsibilities (Blau, 1974; Emerson, 1962; Homans, 1974; Thibaut & Kelley, 1959). Clearly, such an assumption ignores the individual's motivational state. Because all employees do not have the identical salient needs, the indiscriminate adoption of the participative technique does not enhance the leader's effectiveness. On the other hand, the participative leader behavior is effective when the workers' belief in self-determination (Deci, 1975) or personal self-efficacy (Bandura, 1986) is high.

The explicit use of cultural variables to study their influence on the participative leadership role has been explored in two empirical studies. One is a study of U.S. and European managers (Jago et al., 1993). It found that participation scores were higher for low-power-distance cultures than for high-power-distance cultures. The other is a study of U.S. and Turkish super-visors (Kenis, 1977). The findings of this study were also similar: Supervisors in low-power and low-uncertainty-avoidance cultures are more likely to en-gage in participative decision making than those in high-power and high-uncertainty-avoidance cultures. Using the Kanungo and Jaeger (1990) model discussed earlier (Figure 6.1), Mendonca and Kanungo (1994) explained the effect of the sociocultural environment of developing countries and of the internal work culture on the adoption of participative management in organi-zations in these countries. According to the model, the sociocultural dimensions of high uncertainty, low individualism, high power distance, low masculinity, and high context-sensitive thinking are likely to inhibit participative leadership because the attitudes and behaviors that result from these characteristics are incompatible with participative decision making. This incompatibility is further aggravated by the organization's internal work culture, which results from management's descriptive assumptions about human nature, and their normative or prescriptive assumptions about the guiding principles of human conduct. In the paragraphs that follow, we first consider the influence of sociocultural variables and then the influence of the internal work culture on participative leadership effectiveness in developing country organizations.

Impact of Sociocultural Variables

The characteristic of high uncertainty avoidance induces subordinates to be reluctant to exercise autonomy and accept responsibility, which, in turn, leads the manager to exercise greater control and provide more detailed directions than are actually required. In low-individualism cultures, family concerns and group achievements take precedence over the individual's work concerns and achievements. Because the accomplishment of job objectives is not the primary preoccupation of employees, they will not desire to be involved in the decision making related to their job tasks. The high-power-distance characteristic reflects the societal norm that inequality, expressed in status differentials, is part of the human condition. In the organizational context, it implies that managers and subordinates accept and operate from their respective positions in the hierarchy, and the subordinate's obedience and compliance is not based on a rationale of expertise or competence, but simply on the authority inherent in the manager's hierarchical position. Such status differentials do not promote participative decision making.

The low-masculinity characteristic, with its strong emphasis on sensitivity to people and relationships, implies that the satisfaction of affiliative needs, which are more salient than the need to achieve, takes precedence over satisfaction derived from meeting job objectives. Consequently, low masculinity inhibits the effective implementation of participative management, which presupposes that employees seek to fulfill their growth needs on the job through the exercise of control and responsibility on the job, completion of meaningful tasks, and task-relevant interactions. The high-associative or context-sensitive thinking will also inhibit the effectiveness of the participative leadership role because this cultural characteristic implies that individuals' behavior is determined not by the logic of principles, but by the needs of the context that is salient to them. The salient context might be attending to one's personal and social obligations during work hours even at the cost of neglecting one's job tasks and responsibilities.

Impact of Internal Work Culture

When managers assume that their subordinates' locus of control is external, they will logically conclude that their subordinates do not have much confidence in their ability to control events and outcomes and that subordinates will be reluctant to exercise autonomy, to accept responsibility for problem solving, and generally to be involved in decision making. In the context of such assumed reluctance, managers will believe it to be futile to practice participative leadership. The same reluctance to practice participative leadership results from managers' assumption that their subordinates have limited potential and that they are not easily amenable to change and development. Believing that their subordinates do not have high job-related growth needs, managers will not put in the developmental effort to prepare subordinates for participative decision making. The past and present orientation, rather than a future orientation, and a short-term, rather than a long-term, perspective, influenced by the highly unpredictable and uncontrollable economic and political events (Triandis, 1984), also inhibit participative leadership. With such a time orientation and perspective, one is not inclined to invest effort, time, and resources whose returns cannot be realized in the short term. Participative management, and the resulting participative leadership role, essentially requires a future orientation.

The passive or reactive stance to job tasks, largely the effects of low-masculinity and low-individualism characteristics of the sociocultural environment, is also not compatible with participative management, which calls for a proactive or assertive task orientation to assume control and responsibility for goal setting, decision making, problem solving, and initiating appropriate measures to bring about the needed organizational change. The authoritarian and paternalistic norm, which reflects the high power distance that prevails in the sociocultural environment, is not conducive to participative leadership for the same reasons as high power distance, discussed earlier in this section. The last normative assumption that characterizes the internal work culture of developing countries is to allow the exigencies of the situation to determine one's behavior. This norm that behavior be context dependent reflects the associative thinking characteristic of the prevailing sociocultural environment, and carries with it the identical adverse effect on participative management.

Clearly, participative management cannot be *imposed* in an organization irrespective of the sociocultural environment in which the organization operates. The success of participative management depends on the employees' motivational state, which, in turn, is largely the result of the employees' belief in self-determination (Deci, 1975) or their personal self-efficacy belief (Bandura, 1986). When employees do not feel capable of coping with the demands of participative management, they will not be motivated to engage in it. The preceding discussion has demonstrated that, other things being equal, the sociocultural environment of developing countries is not conducive to participative management. In addition, the success of participative management depends on the managers' willingness to engage their subordinates in this mode—that is, to allow them to exercise autonomy and responsibility in relation to their job tasks. The managers' descriptive and prescriptive assumptions about human nature and work behavior, which generally characterize the internal work culture of developing country organizations, would suggest that they are unlikely to engage in the participative management mode.

In these circumstances, participative leadership becomes a viable option for developing countries only to the extent and degree to which its implementation modalities address the cultural constraints and build on the cultural facilitators. The nurturant-task leadership model and related process proposed by Sinha (1990) demonstrates how managers can exercise the participative role by building on the cultural facilitators. For instance, the model (see Figure 6.2) postulates that subordinates can be developed to a state of preparedness for participative management—even to the point of functioning as autonomous work groups. However, the model does not propose strategies to overcome the constraints of high power distance and the authoritarian and paternalistic norms that, it recognizes, might prevent managers from fully adopting the participative mode. The cultural contingencies of the charismatic leadership role, discussed in the next section, provide a much more comprehensive treatment of strategies both to build on the cultural facilitators and to overcome the cultural constraints.

Influence of Culture on the Charismatic Leader Role

The charismatic leadership role has not yet been studied systematically in the cross-cultural context. However, the recent emergence of a model of charismatic leader role behavior (Conger & Kanungo, 1988a) has made the cross-cultural analysis of this leadership role possible. Furthermore, as the following discussion argues, the behavioral content of this role is absolutely critical for organizational leaders in developing countries. The reason is two-fold. First, the behavior exhibited in this role is today considered as exemplary expressions of missionary or change-oriented rather than the supervisory or status quo-oriented leadership. Second, this role is associated with societal and organizational change of a more radical nature. The magnitude of problems that developing countries face today dictates that it is precisely these parts of the world that can ill-afford the luxury of maintaining the status quo; they do indeed have the greatest need for transformation and radical change. The charismatic leadership role has the greatest potential for significant change and development and, therefore, is the role that is eminently suitable for organizational leaders in developing countries.

In discussing the influence of culture on the charismatic leadership role, we shall use the three-stage charismatic leadership process model of Conger and Kanungo (1988a), which has been described in Chapter 2.

▧ CHARISMATIC OR TRANSFORMATIONAL LEADERSHIP: THE ISSUE OF CULTURAL FIT

Besides the complex and unpredictable economic, legal, and political environments of developing countries, a number of sociocultural dimensions will operate as contingency variables for leader effectiveness. As suggested by Kanungo and Jaeger (1990), developing countries tend to be high on power distance (hierarchical social structure and authoritarian socialization practices), high on collectivistic orientation (extended kinship networks), and high on religious traditionalism (a moral and reactive rather than a pragmatic and proactive orientation). This constellation of sociocultural features influences the nature of leadership and supervisory behavior, and the leader-follower relationship. For this reason, the mode of implementing the charismatic leadership must build on the cultural facilitators and overcome the cultural constraints—more specifically discussed in the sections that follow.

The authoritarian socialization practices in developing countries make the relationship between leaders and their followers more personalized rather than contractual. The nature of this personalized relationship can take two distinct forms: (a) affective reciprocity or (b) manipulative ingratiation. A relationship characterized by affective reciprocity manifests itself in the leader's affectionate and nurturant behavior toward followers and in the followers' deference and loyalty to the leader. Furthermore, an affective reciprocity relationship often builds an inner strength and self-efficacy among followers because of the supportive coaching influence of the leader. This type of relationship is conducive to achieving both personal and organizational objectives. A relationship characterized by manipulative ingratiation, on the other hand, is manifested through a superficial affection for followers on the leader's part, but underlying it is a basic distrust of the followers. In return, followers similarly exhibit a superficial loyalty but experience more deeply a sense of rejection of and animosity toward the leader. As a result, manipulative ingratiation develops in followers a fragile self-esteem and ego-defensive tendencies. This type of relationship only fosters the desire to achieve personal goals at the cost of organizational goals.

Sinha (1980) suggested that the affective-reciprocity type of relationship is observed among supervisors who exhibit nurturant-task leadership styles. However, as noted earlier, the nurturant-task leadership process envisages the possibility of the leader regressing to the authoritarian mode. This is so because, as the process gets under way, the leader might feel or sense a loss of control over the followers' actions because of a lack of confidence and trust in them. On the other hand, as it will soon become clear, in the charismatic leadership process, the initiative for the development of the affective-reciprocity relationship originates and rests with the leader. The charismatic leadership process identifies the conditions under which the affective-reciprocity relationship is successful and the strategies the leader needs to adopt in order to promote and strengthen this relationship. Thus, an essential condition is the development of the personal self-efficacy beliefs of the subordinates. For this purpose, the leader must first demonstrate confidence in the followers' ability to handle various tasks (Eden, 1990) and then use empowering strategies such as coaching, modeling, stating performance goals as worthy ideals, and encouraging and rewarding excellence in performance (Conger & Kanungo, 1988d).

The charismatic leader would not engage in strategies that characterize the manipulative-ingratiation relationship, for example, the use of "lording" strategies. In these strategies, the nature of the leadership influence process is chiefly transactional. Thus, the leader literally "extracts" follower compliance in exchange for rewards and sanctions, places an excessive emphasis on followers' performance failures to foster follower dependence, and conceals or restricts the flow of information to retain control over followers. The ultimate effect of lording strategies is to create the followers' dependence on the leader and to ensure their personal loyalty without any regard for, and often at the total neglect of, the organization's objectives. On the other hand, the leadership influence process that underlies empowering strategies is transformational. As in all leadership, the followers do come to depend on the charismatic leader, but such dependence is for the purpose of increasing their task competence and their personal growth and development. Moreover, the loyalty to the leader is motivated by the followers' commitment to the organization's vision and its objectives, which they have internalized and for which they accept ownership.

The second contingency variable for leadership effectiveness is the collectivistic orientation among organizational members in developing countries, which creates a family ethos of embeddedness in kinship or social networks. This results in a strong "we-group" and "they-group" identity, and the associated feelings of trust of the we-group members and distrust for the they-group members. In managerial and leadership practices, such attitudes can inevitably translate into nepotism or favoritism and discrimination in recruitment, selection, performance evaluation, and promotion. It is not long before the organization experiences the dysfunctional effects of these practices, for example, the development among employees of the belief that rewards and outcomes, generally, are not contingent on performance, and the even more serious consequence of employees' experiencing feelings of powerlessness, which invariably results in employee alienation (Ashforth, 1989; Kanungo, 1990). The problems faced by the leaders in such situations are (a) how to bring about the integration of organizational members who belong to various kinship or social groups and (b) how to reduce worker alienation.

The problem of integration can be resolved by the use of a family metaphor for organizations: "This company is one big family in which we are responsible for each other." In addition, embeddedness can be enhanced through opportunities for active participation and teamwork. Of course, the foundation for these efforts is to ensure the process of open communications. The problem of work alienation can be reduced by the idealization of organizational and work values, through organizational socialization practices, and by setting up performance-contingent reward systems. A sense of belonging to an organization as a family is created among followers when they find that the leader is (a) impartial, that is, fair and firm; (b) open, available, and accessible; (c) concerned with improving their quality of work life; (d) sociable and collegial with them and their families; and (e) respectful and supportive of the authority and position of others, particularly those in the second-line positions of executive succession (Singh & Bhandarkar, 1990).

The leader has to act as a role model and set examples through deeds and actions to demonstrate his or her desire and interest in integrating all employees as members of the "one" organization. A recent study of chief executives of five Indian organizations (Singh & Bhandarkar, 1990) supports the contention that the strategies of using the family metaphor, *kutumbization* (one undivided community), and empowerment techniques are the key to successful organizational transformation. A list of behaviors necessary for charismatic leadership effectiveness in developing countries, consistent with the preceding discussion, is presented in Table 6.1.

Finally, religious traditionalism noticed in many developing countries may operate as a cultural contingency variable for charismatic leadership effectiveness. The religious traditions in these countries are highly valued and often determine a leader's judgment of what path of action is morally right or wrong in a given situation. Such judgments have a strong influence in guiding the leader's behavior. The influence of traditional religions and moral norms such as a concern for altruism, high femininity or caring and affiliative concerns, and low masculinity or competitive and acquisitive concerns are often considered to be inimical to the business interests of organizations (Hofstede, 1980; Kanungo & Conger, 1990; Weber, 1958b).

It is argued that the tendency of leaders in developing countries to be guided by moral rather than by pragmatic business considerations has a detrimental effect on public and private sector organizations, chiefly because it ignores or neglects the organization's objectives. This argument, however, is not entirely valid, and indeed highly questionable. Many leaders in developing countries were effective primarily because of their ability to integrate traditional religious and moral values with practical considerations for achieving the future goals of their organizations (Woycke, 1990). Even in Western industrialized countries, it is becoming increasingly evident that organizational leadership needs to have a moral and spiritual base (Kanungo & Conger, 1990; Kanungo & Mendonca, 1994) because without an ethical and altruistic perspective, the very survival of the business over the long term is in serious jeopardy.

Therefore, to be effective, charismatic leaders in developing countries need to provide moral leadership by integrating traditional religious values with pragmatic considerations. The traditional values can be incorporated in the

Table 6.1　Charismatic Leadership Behavior for Developing Countries

1. Assess the environment

   Identify factors that facilitate or hinder achievement of organizational goals

   Assess minimum conditions needed for implementing short- and long-term goals

   Prepare a stakeholder transaction matrix

2. Visioning and responding to the environment

   Establish dominant goal and direct efforts to achieve it

   Move from pilot testing to implementation on a larger scale

   Mobilize demand

   Develop support network

3. Means to achieve

   Establish affective reciprocity relationship

   　　confidence in follower's ability of task accomplishment

   　　nurturing follower self-efficacy through coaching, modeling, encouraging, and rewarding

   　　idealizing organizational and work values

   Discourage manipulative ingratiation relationships

   　　avoid lording behavior and pulling rank

   　　avoid negativism

   　　avoid favoritism

   Promote performance-based reward system

   Promote loyalty to organization and work values rather than loyalty to people in positions of power

   Recognize dependence of subordinates for developing task competence versus dependence for material gain. Be supportive of subordinates in the former case

   Use a family metaphor for organizations

   　　be fair and firm to all members

   　　be open, available, and accessible

   　　be sociable and collegial to members (use existing rites and rituals as occasions for relating to members)

   　　show constant concern for improving quality of life of members as one would do for own self

   　　groom second in command

   　　show respect and support for others' position and authority

   　　promote information sharing, participation, and communication

idealization and articulation of future visions or goals. Furthermore, because these values are cherished by the people at large, the leader's commitment to and practice of these values would have two desirable effects. The first is that the leader's espousal of these values contributes to a greater follower acceptance of the leader's vision. The second effect that results when the leader lives and leads by these values is the followers' perception of congruence between what is espoused and practiced by the leader. As a result, the leader's credibility is greatly enhanced, and, equally important, the leader serves as a role model for the followers.

In their study of transformational corporate leaders in India, Singh and Bhandarkar (1990) concluded:

> A dramatic illustration of this cultural imperative in recent times is Mahatma Gandhi, who could unify and organize the diverse masses. Living by ideals is thus the value that is most cherished by people at large, and they desire to see these values more in their leaders, although they themselves may not necessarily practice them. To take care of the above, the change process must be characterized by role modelling, sincerity, and commitment on the part of the top management, and consistency between precept and practice. (p. 317)

It is recognized that religious traditionalism may create two opposite sets of belief or value systems that form the basis of desirable behaviors in some leaders, and undesirable behaviors in other leaders. Thus, in some leaders it may create a system of beliefs that includes beliefs in heterogeneity and inequality among people—such as the belief in the caste and clan systems, the we- and they-groups, and an external locus of control, fatalism, and destiny—for example, as influenced by the doctrine of *karma* practiced in India. Other possible beliefs might include a preoccupation with the past or the absence of a futuristic orientation, or a sense of time being eternal or ever-present and never passing. Such beliefs make the leader ineffective in achieving organizational objectives. A leader who believes in "inequality" often engages in patronage, favoritism, and discrimination (Virmani & Guptam, 1991). Fatalism and the lack of a futuristic orientation make the leader incapable of visioning and planning to achieve task goals within targeted time periods.

Although such dysfunctional effects can be observed in some leaders, there are other leaders in whom the same religious traditionalism produces an opposite set of beliefs that have positive effects. Influenced by traditionalism, these leaders develop a system of beliefs that emphasizes, as all religions do, heterogeneity and the essential equality among human beings; internal self-control as they cope with environmental demands, which is also an element of the karma doctrine that requires one to be responsible for one's actions; and a healthy optimism for the future. Leaders in non-Western cultures who interpret religious traditionalism in this way tend to implement more effectively the transformational strategies of idealizing the future vision, exercising moral influence, becoming role models, and empowering the followers.

☒ ETHICS OF LEADERSHIP MOTIVATION AND INFLUENCE PROCESSES: CONGRUENCE WITH NON-WESTERN CULTURAL NORMS AND VALUES

The discussion of the ethical dimensions in leadership motivation and leadership influence processes strongly argued that the nature, characteristics, and leader behaviors of the transformational mode of leadership are consistent with the altruistic ethic. The question that arises when we consider the cultural contingencies of leadership is whether the cultural norms and values that prevail in non-Western societies are compatible with the moral values that are inherent in the altruistic ethic. To address this question, we first draw some lessons from the cross-cultural studies in leadership discussed in this chapter. We then explore the values inherent in the basic religions and moral paradigms that are dominant in non-Western societies. Such an exploration is necessary because in traditional societies, these paradigms have been, and still are, the major forces that pervade the socialization of societal members; influence their norms, orientations, and behaviors; and help to explain the social institutions and structures.

The cross-cultural studies (Mendonca & Kanungo, 1994; Sinha, 1990), which explicitly used cultural variables to examine leader effectiveness, suggest that the task, social, and participative leader roles are effective in non-Western societies only to the extent that the roles are performed in the nurturant-task leadership mode. Now, the task, social, and participative leaders, as discussed in Chapter 4, use mainly the transactional influence process. But the focus of the nurturant-task leader is the growth and development of both the followers and the leader. The nurturant-task leadership model postulates that subordinates can be developed to a state of preparedness in order to function autonomously. This "other" focus implies the use of the transformational influence process and, in that sense, the nurturant-task leadership model reflects the altruistic ethic. However, the nurturant-task model recognizes that as it succeeds in developing subordinates to become autonomous, it might, at the same time, cause the leader to resort to the transactional influence process and related control strategies because of the leader's fear that without his or her direction and control, productivity would be compromised. This focus on others of the nurturant-task leader would seem to be purely instrumental in attaining the leader's objective, and for this reason, it would tend to reflect more of the utilitarian or mutual altruism, rather than moral altruism.

Nevertheless, cross-cultural studies show that the task, social, and participative leader roles and the related transactional influence process are inappropriate, and the nurturant-task leader role is appropriate for non-Western cultures. These findings suggest two reasonable inferences. First, the egotistic values implicit in the control strategies of transactional leadership are generally incongruent with the cultural norms and values of these cultures. Second, the altruistic values, although of the utilitarian type, implicit in the development strategies of nurturant-task leadership, are congruent with the cultural norms and values of non-Western cultures.

However, the congruence of moral altruism with the cultural norms and values of non-Western cultures is much more clearly and convincingly demonstrated by the discussion, in the preceding section, of the culture fit of charismatic leadership. It will be noted from that discussion that the charismatic leader's empowering strategies, which reflect the altruistic values and ethics, can be implemented in a manner that is effective and, at the same time, consistent with the moral and ethical values in non-Western cultures, which are briefly presented in the next section.

From ancient times, people have turned to religion to understand the human condition and to seek answers to questions such as:

> What is a man? What is the meaning and purpose of our life? What is goodness and what is sin? What gives rise to our sorrows and to what intent? Where lies the path to true happiness? What is the truth about death, judgement, and retribution beyond the grave? What, finally, is that ultimate and unutterable mystery which engulfs our being, and whence we take our rise, and wither our journey leads us? (Second Vatican Council, 1965, p. 661)

Although the major religions that have shaped the cultural norms and values of non-Western societies might have different and even contradictory theological insights and responses to these questions, there is a remarkable consensus on the ethics of human behavior. It would seem as if the norms of moral behavior are deeply ingrained in human nature. And the underlying thrust of such norms is that the individual's growth and development comes about not when the individual seeks his or her own interests, but rather when the individual strives, even at great pain, risk, or inconvenience to the individual, to seek the good of the other—whether that other be a friend or foe or stranger.

In India, the Hindu way of life exhorts individuals to view themselves as instruments of the divine will, born to engage in moral duties that benefit the social order at the cost of considerable personal sacrifice (Buck, 1978). According to the Vedanta, the most influential school of Hindu thought, the ideal life is a process of growing to be nonegotistic, equananimous, stable-minded persons (Srinivas, 1994). Similar expressions of the altruistic ideal are found in Islam. For example, some of the deeply cherished values of Arab society are "commitments to honour, honesty, respect to parents and older persons, loyalty to primary group, hospitality and generosity" (Ali & Azim, 1994). These values clearly suggest that in Islam, one's personal goals and interests ought not be pursued to the detriment of the goals and interests of the group or community.

The concept of the more inclusive self—that is, one in which the desires of the individual are subordinated to the needs of the larger community, is also found in Buddhism and Confucianism. Thus, one Buddhist sect is known to emphasize personal sacrifice and service to others (Smart, 1983). In a similar vein, Confucianism depicts individuals as embedded in a larger social order with a set of obligations to define themselves in relation to others and to foster harmony in their relations (Ho, 1985; Tuan, 1982). The knowledge that society's well-being ought to supersede one's own well-being is inherent in the nature of human beings, but its development is affected by the socialization process. In this process, the individuals' spiritual experiences that stem from their religious beliefs and practices serve to further reinforce altruistic behavior. Therefore, the religious influences that characterize non-Western societies will serve to hinder the effectiveness of the transactional leadership mode and facilitate the effectiveness of the transformational leadership mode.

"Am I my brother's keeper?" This question, explicitly raised in the Judeo-Christian scriptures, is also echoed in the scriptures and literature of other religious and cultural traditions. Indeed, in every age and in every culture, the tapestry of human life and living is greatly enriched and made more vibrant by the thread of concern for others before concern for one's self. It is, therefore, not surprising that leaders whose lives have left a profound, beneficial influence on their followers—in their own day and today continue to be models for others to emulate—are those who have been true to the noble ideal so well expressed by John Ruskin: "That man is richest who, having perfected the functions of his own life to the utmost, has also the widest helpful influence, both personal, and by means of his possessions, over the lives of others" (quoted in Bartlett, 1968, p. 698).

▧ CONCLUSION

The major thrust of the discussion in this chapter was to examine the culture fit of the four major leadership roles relative to the sociocultural characteristics of developing countries and the internal work culture of organizations in these countries. We discussed the impact of cultural contingencies on the effectiveness of each role. However, keeping in mind that bringing about change or coping with change is *the* dominant and urgent need for organizations in developing countries, the charismatic leadership role emerged as the most appropriate and critical for organizational leaders in these countries. Organizational change is the essence of development. Hence, organizations in developing countries need change more than the maintenance of the status quo.

Bringing about effective changes requires the initiative, guidance, and effort of charismatic leaders—particularly in the development of appropriate strategies on three fronts: (a) an environmental assessment, (b) visioning and responding to the complexities of the environment, and (c) member ingratiation using a family metaphor and member empowerment to achieve organizational goals. The chapter considered the cultural variables that are derived from authoritarianism, collectivism, and traditionalism and that might facilitate or hinder these efforts and proposed specific strategies to build on the cultural facilitators and overcome the cultural constraints.

The chapter also examined the norms and values that pervade the developing non-Western societies and concluded that these are congruent with the altruistic ethic that underlies the transformational leadership process.

References

Abramson, L. Y., Garber, J., & Seligman, M. E. P. (1980). Learned helplessness in humans: An attributional analysis. In J. Garber & M. E. P. Seligman (Eds.), *Human helplessness: Theory and applications* (pp. 3-34). New York: Academic Press.

Adler, M. J. (1981). *Six great ideas.* New York: Macmillan.

Ali, J. A., & Azim, A. (1994, July). *Islamic work ethic and organizational development.* Paper presented at the 23rd International Congress of Applied Psychology, Madrid, Spain.

Andrews, K. R. (1989, September-October). Ethics in practice. *Harvard Business Review,* pp. 99-104.

Andriessen, E. J. H., & Drenth, P. J. D. (1984). Leadership: Theories and models. In P. J. D. Drenth, H. Thierry, P. J. Willems, & C. J. de Wolff (Eds.), *Handbook of work and organizational psychology* (pp. 481-520). New York: John Wiley.

Ashforth, B. E. (1989). The experience of powerlessness in organizations. *Organizational Behavior and Human Decision Processes, 43,* 207-242.

Avolio, B. J., & Bass, B. M. (1988). Transformational leadership, charisma, and beyond. In J. G. Hunt, B. R. Baliga, H. P. Dachler, & C. A. Schriesheim (Eds.), *Emerging leadership vistas* (pp. 29-49). Lexington, MA: D. C. Heath.

Bakan, D. (1966). *The duality of human existence.* Chicago: Rand McNally.

Bales, R. F., & Slater, P. E. (1955). Role differentiation in small decision-making groups. In T. Parson & R. F. Bales (Eds.), *Family, socialization, and interaction process* (pp. 259-306). Glencoe, IL: Free Press.

Bandura, A. (1977). Self-efficacy: Toward a unifying theory of behavioral change. *Psychological Review, 84,* 191-215.

Bandura, A. (1986). *Social foundations of thought and action: A social-cognitive view.* Englewood Cliffs, NJ: Prentice Hall.

Barry, V. (1978). *Personal and social ethics*. Belmont, CA: Wadsworth.

Bartlett, J. (1968). *Familiar quotations: A collection of passages, phrases, and proverbs traced to their sources in ancient and modern literature*. Boston: Little, Brown.

Bass, B. M. (1985). *Leadership performance beyond expectations*. New York: Academic Press.

Bass, B. M. (1988). Evolving perspectives on charismatic leadership. In J. A. Conger & R. N. Kanungo (Eds.), *Charismatic leadership: The elusive factor in organizational effectiveness* (pp. 40-77). San Francisco: Jossey-Bass.

Bass, B. M. (1990a). *Bass and Stogdill's handbook of leadership* (3rd ed.). New York: Free Press.

Bass, B. M. (1990b, Winter). From transactional to transformational leadership: Learning to share the vision. *Organizational Dynamics*, pp. 19-32.

Bass, B. M., & Burger P. C. (1979). *Assessment of managers: An international comparison*. New York: Free Press.

Baumeister, R. (1987). How the self became a problem: A psychological review of historical research. *Journal of Personality and Social Psychology, 52*, 163-176.

Baumhart, R. (1968). *Ethics in business*. New York: Holt, Rinehart & Winston.

Bennis, W. G. (1959). Leadership theory and administrative behavior: The problem of authority. *Administrative Science Quarterly, 4*, 259-301.

Bennis, W. G., & Nanus, B. (1985). *Leaders*. New York: Harper & Row.

Berenbeim, R. E. (1987). *Corporate ethics*. New York: Conference Board, Inc.

Berkowitz, L. (1972). Social norms, feelings, and other factors affecting helping and altruism. In L. Berkowitz (Ed.), *Advances in experimental psychology* (pp. 63-108). New York: Academic Press.

Bettelheim, B. (1943). Individual and mass behavior in extreme situations. *Journal of Abnormal and Social Psychology, 38*, 417-452.

Blake, R. R., & Mouton, J. S. (1964). *The managerial grid*. Houston: Gulf.

Blanchard, K., & Peale, N. V. (1988). *The power of ethical management*. New York: Fawcett Crest.

Blau, P. M. (1974). *Exchange and power in social life*. New York: John Wiley.

Blauner, R. (1964). *Alienation and freedom*. Chicago: University of Chicago Press.

Block, J. (1973). Conception of sex roles: Some cross-cultural and longitudinal perspectives. *American Psychologist, 28*, 512-526.

Block, P. (1987). *The empowered manager*. San Francisco: Jossey-Bass.

Bond, M. H., & Hwang, K. K. (1986). The social psychology of Chinese people. In M. H. Bond (Ed.), *The psychology of the Chinese people* (pp. 213-266). Hong Kong: Oxford University Press.

Boyatzis, R. E. (1973). Affiliation motivation. In D. McClelland (Ed.), *Human motivation: A book of readings* (pp. 252-278). Morristown, NJ: General Learning Press.

Boyatzis, R. E. (1982). *The competent manager: A model for effective performance.* New York: John Wiley.

Boyatzis, R. E. (1984). The need for close relationships and the manager's job. In D. A. Kolb, I. M. Rubin, & J. M. McIntyre (Eds.), *Organizational psychology: Readings on human behavior in organizations* (pp. 81-86). Englewood Cliffs, NJ: Prentice Hall.

Braden, W. (1970). *The age of Aquarius.* Chicago: Quadrangle Books.

Bradley, R. T. (1987). *Charisma and social structure: A study of love and power, wholeness and transformation.* New York: Paragon.

Brief, A. P., & Motowidlo, S. J. (1986). Prosocial organizational behaviors. *Academy of Management Review, 11,* 710-725.

Bryman, A. (1986). *Leadership and organizations.* London: Routledge & Kegan Paul.

Buck, W. (1978). *Ramayana.* New York: New American Library.

Burke, W. (1986). Leadership as empowering others. In S. Srivastva & Associates, *Executive power: How executives influence people and organizations.* San Francisco: Jossey-Bass.

Burns, J. M. (1978). *Leadership.* New York: Harper & Row.

Bynner, W. (1962). *The way of life according to Lao Tzu.* New York: Capricorn.

Calder, B. J. (1977). An attribution theory of leadership. In B. M. Staw & G. R. Salancik (Eds.), *New directions in organizational behavior.* Chicago: St. Clair.

Campbell, D. (1975, December). On the conflicts between biological and social evolution and between psychology and moral tradition. *American Psychologist, 30,* 1103-1126.

Cartwright, D. (1965). Leadership, influence and control. In J. G. March (Ed.), *Handbook of organizations* (pp. 1-47). Chicago: Rand McNally.

Cartwright, D., & Zander, A. (Eds.). (1968). *Group dynamics: Research and theory.* New York: Harper & Row.

Coch, L., & French, J. R. P., Jr. (1948). Overcoming resistance to change. *Human Relations, 1,* 512-532.

Concise Oxford English dictionary of current English (5th ed.). (1964). London: Oxford University Press.

Conger, J. A. (1985). *Charismatic leadership in business: An exploratory study.* Unpublished doctoral dissertation, Harvard University, School of Business Administration.

Conger, J. A. (1989). *The charismatic leader.* San Francisco: Jossey-Bass.

Conger, J. A. (1990, Winter). The dark side of leadership. *Organizational Dynamics,* pp. 44-55.

Conger, J. A., & Kanungo, R. N. (1987). Toward a behavioral theory of charismatic leadership in organizational settings. *Academy of Management Review, 12,* 637-647.

Conger, J. A., & Kanungo, R. N. (1988a). Behavioral dimensions of charismatic leadership. In J. A. Conger & R. N. Kanungo (Eds.), *Charismatic leadership: The elusive factor in organizational effectiveness* (pp. 78-97). San Francisco: Jossey-Bass.

Conger, J. A., & Kanungo, R. N. (Eds.). (1988b). *Charismatic leadership: The elusive factor in organizational effectiveness.* San Francisco: Jossey-Bass.

Conger, J. A., & Kanungo, R. N. (1988c). The empowerment process: Integrating theory and practice. *Academy of Management Review, 13,* 471-482.

Conger, J. A., & Kanungo, R. N. (1988d). Patterns and trends in studying charismatic leadership. In J. A. Conger & R. N. Kanungo (Eds.), *Charismatic leadership: The elusive factor in organizational effectiveness* (pp. 324-336). San Francisco: Jossey-Bass.

Conger, J. A., & Kanungo, R. N. (1992). Perceived behavioral attributes of charismatic leadership. *Canadian Journal of Behavioral Sciences, 24,* 86-102.

Conger, J. A., & Kanungo, R. N. (1994). Charismatic leadership in organizations: Perceived behavioral attributes and their measurement. *Journal of Organizational Behavior, 15,* 439-452.

Cowley, W. H. (1928). Three distinctions in the study of leaders. *Journal of Abnormal and Social Psychology, 23,* 144-157.

Daboub, A. J., Rasheed, A. M. A., Priem, R. L., & Gray, D. A. (1995). Top management team characteristics and corporate illegal activity. *Academy of Management Review, 20,* 138-170.

Dahl, R. A. (1957). The concept of power. *Behavioral Science, 2,* 201-218.

Dawes, R. (1975). Formal models of dilemmas in social-decision making. In M. Kaplan & S. Schwartz (Eds.), *Human judgment and decision processes.* New York: Academic Press.

Deci, E. L. (1975). *Intrinsic motivation.* New York: Plenum.

Deutsch, M. (1973). *The resolution of conflict: Constructive and destructive processes.* New Haven, CT: Yale University Press.

Dorfman, P. W. (1994, April). *Cross cultural leadership research: Issues and assumptions.* Paper presented at the SIDP conference symposium, Nashville, TN.

Downton, J. V., Jr. (1973). *Rebel leadership.* New York: Free Press.

Drucker, P. F. (1968). *The practice of management.* London: Pan Books.

Dyer, W. (1977). *Team building.* Reading, MA: Addison-Wesley.

Earley, P. C. (1993). East meets West meets Mideast: Further explorations of collectivistic and individualistic work groups. *Academy of Management Journal, 36,* 319-348.

Eden, D. (1990). Industrialization as a self-fulfilling prophecy: The role of expectations in development. *International Journal of Psychology, 25,* 871-886.

Emerson, R. M. (1962). Power-dependence relations. *American Sociological Review, 27,* 31-41.

Erez, M. (1994). Toward a model of cross-cultural industrial and organizational psychology. In H. C. Triandis, M. D. Dunnette, & L. M. Hough (Eds.), *Handbook of industrial and organizational psychology* (Vol. 4, pp. 559-608). Palo Alto, CA: Consulting Psychologists Press.

Etzioni, A. (1989, September 18). Money, power, and fame. *Newsweek,* p. 10.

Evans, M. G. (1970). The effects of supervisory behavior on the path-goal relationship. *Organizational Behavior and Human Performance, 5,* 277-298.

The executive as a social activist. (1970, July 20). *Time,* p. 50.

Fiedler, F. E. (1967). *A theory of leadership effectiveness.* New York: McGraw-Hill.

Fiedler, F. E, & Chemers, M. M. (1974). *Leadership and effective management.* Glenview, IL: ScottForesman.

Fleishman, E. A., Harris, E. F., & Burtt, H. E. (1955). *Leadership and supervision in industry.* Columbus: Ohio State University, Bureau of Educational Research.

Flinn, J. (1995, March 25). Don't get sucked into management's world, directors told. *Gazette,* p. C2. (Montreal)

French, J. R. P., Jr., & Raven, B. (1959). The bases of social power. In D. P. Cartwright (Ed.), *Studies in social power* (pp. 150-167). Ann Arbor, MI: Institute for Social Research.

Freud, A. (1946). *The ego and the mechanisms of defense.* New York: International Universities Press.

Friedman, M. (1963). *Capitalism and freedom.* Chicago: University of Chicago Press.

Fullinwider, R. K. (1986, Summer). Civic education and traditional values. *Philosophy and Public Policy.*

Galanter, M. (1982). Charismatic religious sects and psychiatry: An overview. *American Journal of Psychiatry, 139,* 1539-1548.

Galbraith, J. (1967). *The new industrial state.* Boston: Houghton Mifflin.

Garber, J., & Seligman, M. E. P. (Eds.). (1980). *Human helplessness: Theory and applications.* Orlando, FL: Academic Press.

George, J. M., & Brief, A. P. (1992). Feeling good—doing good: A conceptual analysis of the mood at work-organizational spontaneity relationship. *Psychological Bulletin, 112,* 310-329.

Glenn, E. S., & Glenn, C. G. (1981). *Man and mankind: Conflict and communication between cultures.* Norwood, NJ: Ablex.

Gouldner, A. (1960). The norm of reciprocity: A preliminary statement. *American Sociological Review, 25,* 161-178.

Growald, E., & Luks, A. (1988). Beyond self. *American Health, 7,* 51-53.

Haire, M., Ghiselli, E. F., & Porter, L. W. (1966). *Managerial thinking: An international study.* New York: John Wiley.

Halcrow, A. (1987, November). Outlook: Is there a crisis in business ethics? *Personnel Journal,* pp. 10-17.

Halpin, A. W., & Winer, B. J. (1952). *The leadership behavior of the airplane commander.* Columbus: Ohio State University Research Foundation.

Hardin, G. (1968). The tragedy of the commons. *Science, 162,* 1243-1248.

Heller, F. (1971). *Managerial decision making: A study of leadership and power sharing among senior managers.* London: Tavistock.

Hirsch, F. (1976). *Social limits to growth.* Cambridge, MA: Harvard University Press.

Ho, D. (1985). Cultural values and professional issues in clinical psychology: Implications from the Hong Kong experience. *American Psychologist, 40,* 1212-1218.

Hofstede, G. (1980). *Culture's consequences: International differences in work-related values.* Beverly Hills, CA: Sage.

Hofstede, G. (1993). Cultural constraints in management theories. *The Executive, 7,* 81-94.

Hogan, R., Curphy, G. J., & Hogan, J. (1994). What we know about leadership: Effectiveness and personality. *American Psychologist, 49,* 493-504.

Hollander, E. P. (1958). Conformity, status, and idiosyncrasy credit. *Psychological Review, 65,* 117-127.

Hollander, E. P. (1964). *Leaders, groups, and influence.* New York: Oxford University Press.

Hollander, E. P. (1978). *Leadership dynamics.* New York: Free Press.

Hollander, E. P. (1979). Leadership and social exchange processes. In K. Gergen, M. S. Greenberg, & R. H. Willis (Eds.), *Social exchange: Advances in theory and research* (pp. 103-118). New York: Winston-Wiley.

Hollander, E. P. (1986). On the central role of leadership processes. *International Review of Applied Psychology, 35,* 39-52.

Hollander, E. P., & Offermann, L. R. (1990). Power and leadership in organizations. *American Psychologist, 45,* 179-189.

Homans, A. (1974). *Social behavior: Its elementary forms.* New York: Harcourt Brace Jovanovich.

House, R., & Singh, J. (1987). Organizational behavior: Some new directions for I/O psychology. *Annual Review of Psychology, 38,* 669-718.

House, R. J. (1971). A path-goal theory of leadership effectiveness. *Administrative Science Quarterly, 16,* 321-332.

House, R. J. (1977). A 1976 theory of charismatic leadership. In J. G. Hunt & L. L. Larson (Eds.), *Leadership: The cutting edge* (pp. 189-207). Carbondale: Southern Illinois University Press.

House, R. J. (1988a). Leadership research: Some forgotten, ignored, or overlooked findings. In J. G. Hunt, B. R. Baliga, H. P. Dachler, & C. A. Schriesheim (Eds.), *Emerging leadership vistas* (pp. 245-260). Lexington, MA: D. C. Heath.

House, R. J. (1988b). Power and personality in complex organizations. In L. L. Cummings & B. M. Staw (Eds.), *Research in organizational behavior: An annual review of critical essays and reviews* (Vol. 10, pp. 305-357). Greenwich, CT: JAI.

House, R. J., & Dessler, G. (1974). The path-goal theory of leadership: Some post hoc and a priori tests. In J. G. Hunt & L. L. Larson (Eds.), *Contingency approaches to leadership* (pp. 29-55). Carbondale: Southern Illinois University Press.

House, R. J., & Mitchell, T. R. (1974). Path-goal theory of leadership. *Journal of Contemporary Business, 3*(4), 81-97.

House, R. J., Spangler, W. D., & Woycke, J. (1991). Personality and charisma in the U.S. presidency: A psychological theory of leader effectiveness. *Administrative Science Quarterly, 36,* 364-396.

House, R. J., Woycke, J., & Fodor, E. (1988). Charismatic and noncharismatic leaders: Differences in behavior and effectiveness. In J. A. Conger & R. N. Kanungo (Eds.), *Charismatic leadership: The elusive factor in organizational effectiveness* (pp. 98-121). San Francisco: Jossey-Bass.

Howell, J. M. (1988). Two faces of charisma. In J. A. Conger & R. N. Kanungo (Eds.), *Charismatic leadership: The elusive factor in organizational effectiveness* (pp. 213-236). San Francisco: Jossey-Bass.

Howell, J. M., & Avolio, B. J. (1992). The ethics of charismatic leadership: Submission or liberation? *Academy of Management Executive, 6*(2), 43-54.

Hunt, J. G. (1984). Organizational leadership: The contingency paradigm and its challenges. In B. Kellerman (Ed.), *Leadership: Multidisciplinary perspectives* (pp. 113-138). Englewood Cliffs, NJ: Prentice Hall.

Hunt, J. G., Baliga, B. R., Dachler, H. P., & Schriesheim, C. A. (Eds.). (1988). *Emerging leadership vistas.* Lexington, MA: D. C. Heath.

Jackson, D. (1967). *Personality research form manual.* Goshen, NY: Research Psychologists Press.

Jago, A. (1982). Leadership: Perspectives in theory and research. *Management Science, 28,* 315-336.

Jago, A. G., Reber, G., Bohnisch, W., Maczynski, J., Zavrel, J., & Dudorkin, J. (1993, November). *Culture's consequence? A seven nation study of participation.* Paper presented at the meeting of the Decision Sciences Institute, Washington, DC.

Jenkins, C., Rosenman, R., & Zyzanski, S. (1974). Prediction of clinical coronary heart disease by a test for the coronary-prone behavior pattern. *New England Journal of Medicine, 23,* 1271-1275.

John Paul II. (1981). *Encyclical laborem exercens.* Ottawa, Ontario: Canadian Conference of Catholic Bishops.

John Paul II. (1994). *Crossing the threshold of hope.* Toronto, Ontario: Knopf.

Kangas, E. A. (1988). Introduction. In *Ethics in American business: A special report* (pp. 5-14). New York: Touche Ross.

Kanter, R. M. (1979, July-August). Power failure in management circuits. *Harvard Business Review,* pp. 65-75.

Kanter, R. M. (1983). *The change masters.* New York: Simon & Schuster.

Kanungo, R. N. (1977). Bases of supervisory power and job satisfaction in bicultural context. In H. C. Jain & R. N. Kanungo (Eds.), *Behavioral issues in management: The Canadian context* (pp. 331-344). Toronto: McGraw-Hill Ryerson.

Kanungo, R. N. (1982). *Work alienation.* New York: Praeger.

Kanungo, R. N. (1987). Reward management: A new look. In S. Dolan & R. Schuler (Eds.), *Canadian readings and human resource management* (pp. 261-275). St. Paul, MN: West.

Kanungo, R. N. (1990). Culture and work alienation: Western models and Eastern realities. *International Journal of Psychology, 25,* 795-812.

Kanungo, R. N., & Conger, J. A. (1989, July). *Charismatic leadership: A behavioral theory and its cross-cultural implications.* Paper presented at the International Association for Cross-Cultural Psychology Conference, Free University, Amsterdam.

Kanungo, R. N., & Conger, J. A. (1990). The quest for altruism in organizations. In S. Srivastva & D. L. Cooperrider (Eds.), *Appreciative management and leadership* (pp. 288-256). San Francisco: Jossey-Bass.

Kanungo, R. N., & Conger, J. (1993). Promoting altruism as a corporate goal. *Academy of Management Executive, 7*(3), 37-48.

Kanungo, R. N., & Jaeger, A. M. (1990). Introduction: The need for indigenous management in developing countries. In A. M. Jaeger & R. N. Kanungo (Eds.), *Management in developing countries* (pp. 1-19). London: Routledge.

Kanungo, R. N., & Mendonca, M. (1992). *Compensation: Effective reward management.* Toronto, Ontario: Butterworths.

Kanungo, R. N., & Mendonca, M. (1994). *What leaders cannot do without: The spiritual dimensions of leadership.* In J. A. Conger (Ed.), *Spirit at work* (pp. 162-198). San Francisco: Jossey-Bass.

Katz, D., & Kahn, R. (1978). *The social psychology of organizations* (2nd ed.). Toronto, Ontario: Wiley.

Kedia, B. L., & Bhagat, R. S. (1988). Cultural constraints on transfer of technology across nations: Implications for research in international and comparative management. *Academy of Management Review, 13,* 559-571.

Kelman, H. C. (1958). Compliance, identification, and internalization: Three processes of attitude change. *Journal of Conflict Resolution, 2,* 51-60.

Kenis, I. (1977). A cross-cultural study of personality and leadership. *Group and Organization Studies, 2*(1), 49-60.

Kerr, S., & Jermier, J. M. (1978). Substitutes for leadership: Their meaning and measurement. *Organizational Behavior and Human Performance, 22,* 375-403.

Kets de Vries, M. F. R. (1988). Origins of charisma: Ties that bind the leader and the led. In J. A. Conger & R. N. Kanungo (Eds.), *Charismatic leadership: The elusive factor in organizational effectiveness* (pp. 237-252). San Francisco: Jossey-Bass.

Kets de Vries, M. F. R. (1994). The leadership mystique. *Academy of Management Executive, 8*(3), 73-89.

Kohlberg, L. (1969). Stage and sequence: A cognitive-developmental approach to socialization. In D. Goslin (Ed.), *Handbook of socialization theory* (pp. 347-480). Chicago: Rand McNally.

Kramer, R. (1991). *Ed school follies: The miseducation of America's teachers.* New York: Free Press.

Krebs, D. (1982). Altruism: A rational approach. In H. Eizenberg (Ed.), *The development of prosocial behavior* (pp. 53-76). New York: Academic Press.

Kreeft, P. (1990). *Making choices: Practical wisdom for everyday moral decisions.* Ann Arbor, MI: Servant.

Lank, A. G. (1988). The ethical criterion in business decision-making: Optional or imperative. In *Ethics in American business: A special report* (p. 47). New York: Touche Ross.

Lawler, E. E. (1971). *Pay and organizational effectiveness: A psychological view.* New York: McGraw-Hill.

Leavitt, H. (1986). *Corporate pathfinders.* Homewood, IL: Dow Jones-Irwin.

Levinson, H. (1976). *Psychological man.* Cambridge, MA: Levinson Institute.

Levitt, T. (1958). The dangers of social responsibility. *Harvard Business Review, 36*(5), 41-50.

Lewin, K., Lippitt, R., & White, R. K. (1939). Patterns of aggressive behavior in experimentally created social climates. *Journal of Social Psychology, 10,* 271-299.

Likert, R. (1961). *New patterns of management.* New York: McGraw-Hill.

Likert, R. (1967). *The human organization: Its management and value.* New York: McGraw-Hill.

Lippit, R., & White, R. K. (1947). An experimental study of leadership and group life. In E. E. Maccoby, T. M. Newcomb, & E. C. Hartley (Eds.), *Readings in social psychology* (pp. 496-511). New York: Holt, Rinehart & Winston.

Litwin, G. H., & Stringer, R. A., Jr. (1968). *Motivation and organizational climate.* Boston: Harvard Business School, Division of Research.

Locke, E. A., & Latham, G. P. (1984). Goal setting—A motivational technique that works. *Organizational Dynamics, 8*(2), 68-80.

Lodahl, A. (1982). *Crises in values and the success of the Unification Church.* Unpublished B.A. thesis, Cornell University.

Loevinger, J. (1976). *Ego development: Conceptions and theories.* San Francisco: Jossey-Bass.

Luthans, F., & Kreitner, R. (1975). *Organizational behavior modification.* Glenview, IL: ScottForesman.

Macaulay, J., & Berkowitz, L. (1970). Overview. In J. Macaulay & L. Berkowitz (Eds.), *Altruism and helping behavior* (pp. 1-12). New York: Academic Press.

Martinko, M. J., & Gardner, W. L. (1982). Learned helplessness: An alternative explanation for performance deficits. *Academy of Management Review, 7,* 195-204.

Maslow, A. (1965). *Eupsychian management.* Homewood, IL: Irwin.

Maslow, A. (1967). A theory of metamotivation: The biological rootings of the value life. *Journal of Humanistic Psychology, 7,* 108-109.

Maslow, A. (1973). Deficiency motivation and growth motivation. In D. C. McClelland & R. S. Steele (Eds.), *Human motivation: A book of readings* (pp. 233-251). Morristown, NJ: General Learning.

McClelland, D. (1961). *The achieving society.* Princeton, NJ: Van Nostrand.

McClelland, D. (1975). *Power: The inner experience.* New York: John Wiley.

McClelland, D. C. (1985). *Human motivation.* Glenview, IL: ScottForesman.

McClelland, D. C. (1995, January-February). Retrospective commentary. *Harvard Business Review,* pp. 138-139.

McClelland, D. C., & Burnham, D. H. (1995, January-February). Power is the great motivator. *Harvard Business Review,* pp. 126-139.

McGregor, D. (1960). *The human side of enterprise.* New York: McGraw-Hill.

Mehta, P. (1994). Empowering the people for social achievement. In R. N. Kanungo & M. Mendonca (Eds.), *Work motivation: Models for developing countries* (pp. 161-183). New Delhi: Sage.

Meindl, J. R., Ehrlich, S. B., & Dukerich, J. M. (1985). The romance of leadership. *Administrative Science Quarterly, 30,* 78-102.

Mendonca, M., & Kanungo, R. N. (1994). Managing human resources: The issue of cultural fit. *Journal of Management Inquiry, 3,* 189-205.

Mensa chapter sparks furor. (1995, January 11). *Globe and Mail,* p. A6.

Mintzberg, H. (1982a). If you are not serving Bill and Barbara, then you are not serving leadership. In J. G. Hunt, U. Sekaran, & C. A. Schriesheim (Eds.), *Leadership: Beyond establishment views* (pp. 239-259). Carbondale: Southern Illinois University Press.

Mintzberg, H. (1982b). A note on that dirty word, "efficiency." *Interfaces, 12*(5), 101-105.

Mintzberg, H. (1983). *Power in and around organizations.* Englewood Cliffs, NJ: Prentice Hall.

Misumi, J. (1985). *The behavioral science of leadership: An interdisciplinary Japanese research program.* Ann Arbor: University of Michigan Press.

Misumi, J. (1988, November). *The meaning of work (MOW) for the Japanese and action research on small group activities in Japanese industrial organizations.* Paper presented at the International Symposium on Social Values and Effective Organizations, Taipei, Taiwan.

Misumi, J., & Peterson, M. F. (1985). The performance-maintenance (PM) theory of leadership: Review of a Japanese research program. *Administrative Science Quarterly, 30,* 198-223.

Mook, D. (1987). *Motivation: The organization of action.* New York: Norton.

Morris, C. (1972). *The discovery of the individual: 1050-1200.* London: Camelot.

Mowrer, O. H. (1950). *Learning theory and personality dynamics.* New York: Ronald.

Murray, H. (1938). *Explorations in personality.* New York: Oxford University Press.

Nadler, D. A., & Tushman, M. L. (1990, Winter). Beyond the charismatic leader: Leadership and organizational change. *California Management Review,* pp. 77-97.

Neilsen, E. (1986). Empowerment strategies: Balancing authority and responsibility. In S. Srivastva & Associates, *Executive power: How executives influence people and organizations.* San Francisco: Jossey-Bass.

Ohmann, O. A. (1989). Skyhooks. In K. R. Andrews (Ed.), *Ethics in practice: Managing the moral corporation* (pp. 58-69). Boston: Harvard Business School Press.

Oldham, G. R. (1976). The motivation strategies used by supervisors. *Organizational Behavior and Human Performance, 15,* 66-86.

Organ, D. W. (1988). *Organizational citizenship behavior: The good soldier syndrome.* Lexington, MA: Lexington Books.

O'Toole, J. (1985). *Vanguard management: Redesigning the corporate future.* Gorden City, NY: Doubleday.

Ouchi, W. (1981). *Theory Z: How American business can meet the Japanese challenge.* Reading, MA: Addison-Wesley.

Paine, L. S. (1994, March-April). Managing for organizational integrity. *Harvard Business Review,* pp. 106-117.

Pascale, R., & Athos, A. (1981). *The art of Japanese management.* New York: Simon & Schuster.

Peterson, M. F., Maiya, H., & Herreid, C. (1987). *Field application of Japanese PM leadership theory in two US service organizations.* Unpublished manuscript, Texas Technology University, Lubbock, College of Business.

Peterson, M. F., Smith, M. F., & Tayeb, M. H. (1987, November). *Development and use of English-language versions of Japanese PM leadership measures in electronics plants.* Proceedings of the annual meeting of the Southern Management Association, New Orleans.

Pfeffer, J. (1977). The ambiguity of leadership. *Academy of Management Review, 2,* 104-112.

Pfeffer, J. (1981). Management as symbolic action: The creation and maintenance of organizational paradigms. In L. L. Cumming & B. M. Staw (Eds.), *Research in organizational behavior* (Vol. 3, pp. 1-52). Greenwich, CT: JAI.

Podsakoff, P. M., Todor, W. D., & Skov, R. (1982). Effect of leader contingent and non-contingent reward and punishment behaviors on subordinate performance and satisfaction. *Academy of Management Journal, 25,* 810-821.

Radhakrishnan, S. (1962). *The Hindu view of life.* New York: Macmillan.

Reich, C. (1971). *The greening of America: How the youth revolution is trying to make America livable.* New York: Bantam.

Roberts, N. (1985). Transforming leadership: A process of collective action. *Human Relations, 38,* 1023-1046.

Roland, A. (1988). *In search of self in India and Japan: Toward a cross-cultural psychology.* Princeton, NJ: Princeton University Press.

Rothbaum, F. M., Weisz, J. R., & Snyder, S. S. (1982). Changing the world and changing self: A two process model of perceived control. *Journal of Personality and Social Psychology, 42,* 5-37.

Rotter, J. B. (1966). Generalized expectancies for internal versus external control of reinforcement. *Psychological Monographs, 80*(1, Whole No. 609).

Rotter, J., & Stein, D. (1971). Public attitudes toward the trustworthiness, competence, and altruism of twenty selected occupations. *Journal of Applied Social Psychology, 1,* 334-343.

Runciman, W. (1978). *Weber in translation.* Cambridge, MA: Harvard University Press.

Salk, J. (1973). *The survival of the wisest.* New York: Harper & Row.

Sampson, E. (1988). The debate on individualism: Indigenous psychologies of the individual and their role in personal and societal functioning. *American Psychologist, 43,* 15-22.

Sashkin, M. (1984, Spring). Participative management is an ethical imperative. *Organizational Dynamics*, pp. 5-22.

Sashkin, M. (1988). The visionary leader. In J. A. Conger & R. N. Kanungo (Eds.), *Charismatic leadership: The elusive factor in organizational effectiveness* (pp. 122-160). San Francisco: Jossey-Bass.

Schein, E. (1980). *Organizational psychology.* Englewood Cliffs, NJ: Prentice Hall.

Schein, E. H. (1958). The Chinese indoctrination program for prisoners of war: A study of attempted "brainwashing." In E. E. Maccoby, T. M. Newcomb, & E. L. Hartley (Eds.), *Readings in social psychology* (3rd ed., pp. 311-334). New York: Holt.

Schein, E. H. (1985). *Organizational culture and leadership.* San Francisco: Jossey-Bass.

Schermerhorn, J., Hunt, J., & Osborn, R. (1988). *Managing organizational behavior.* New York: John Wiley.

Schmidt, W., & Posner, B. (1983). *Managerial values in perspective.* New York: American Management Association, Membership Publication Division.

Schwartz, B. (1986). *The battle for human nature.* New York: Norton.

Schwartz, B. (1990). The creation and destruction of value. *American Psychologist, 45,* 7-15.

Schwartz, S. (1975). The justice of need and the activation of humanitarian norms. *Journal of Social Issues, 31,* 111-136.

Second Vatican Council. (1963). Pastoral constitution on the church in the modern world. In W. M. Abbott (Ed.), *The documents of Vatican II* (pp. 199-331). New York: Guild Press.

Second Vatican Council. (1965). Declaration on the relationship of the church to non-Christian religions. In W. M. Abbott (Ed.), *The documents of Vatican II* (pp. 660-668). New York: Guild Press.

Shamir, B., House, R. J., & Arthur, M. B. (1989). *The transformational effects of charismatic leadership: A motivational theory.* Working paper, Reginald Jones Center for Strategic Management, Wharton School of Management, Philadelphia.

Shepard, J. M. (1971). *Automation and alienation.* Cambridge: MIT Press.

Simon, H. (1990). A mechanism for social selection and successful altruism. *Science, 250,* 1665-1668.

Sims, H. P. (1977). The leader as manager of reinforcement contingencies: An empirical example and a model. In J. G. Hunt & L. L. Larson (Eds.), *Leadership: The cutting edge* (pp. 121-137). Carbondale: Southern Illinois University Press.

Singh, P., & Bhandarkar, A. (1990). *Corporate success and transformational leadership.* New Delhi: Wiley Eastern.

Sinha, J. B. P. (1980). *The nurturant task leader.* New Delhi: Concept.

Sinha, J. B. P. (1990). A model of effective leadership styles in India. In A. M. Jaeger & R. N. Kanungo (Eds.), *Management in developing countries* (pp. 252-263). London: Routledge.

Smart, N. (1983). *Worldviews: Crosscultural explorations of human beliefs.* New York: Scribner.

Smith, A. (1936). *An inquiry into the nature and wealth of nations.* New York: Modern Library. (Original work published 1776)

Smith, P. B., & Peterson, M. F. (1988). *Leadership, organizations and culture.* London: Sage.

Spaemann, R. (1989). *Basic moral concepts.* London: Routledge.

Spence, J. (1985). Achievement American style: The rewards and costs of individualism. *American Psychologist, 40,* 1285-1295.

Spence, J., & Helmreich, R. (1983). Achievement-related motives and behavior. In J. Spence (Ed.), *Achievement and achievement motives: Psychological approaches* (pp. 7-74). San Francisco: Freeman.

Srinivas, K. M. (1994). Organization development: Maya or Moksha. In R. N. Kanungo & M. Mendonca (Eds.), *Work motivation: Models for developing countries* (pp. 248-282). New Delhi: Sage.

Stovall, R. H. (1988). The Trinity Center roundtable—The ethics of corporate leadership. In *Ethics in American business: A special report* (pp. 28-29). New York: Touche Ross.

Strauss, G. (1977). Managerial practices. In J. R. Hackman & L. J. Suttle (Eds.), *Improving life at work: Behavioral science approaches to organizational change* (pp. 297-363). Santa Monica, CA: Goodyear.

Student, K. R. (1968). Supervisory influence and work-group performance. *Journal of Applied Psychology, 52,* 188-194.

Tannenbaum, R., & Schmidt, W. H. (1958, March-April). How to choose a leadership pattern. *Harvard Business Review.*

Thibaut, J. W., & Kelley, H. H. (1959). *The social psychology of groups.* New York: John Wiley.

Thomas, A. B. (1988). Does leadership make a difference to organizational performance? *Administrative Science Quarterly, 33,* 388-400.

Thomas, K. W., & Velthouse, B. A. (1990). Cognitive elements empowerment: An "interpretive" model of intrinsic task motivation. *Academy of Management Review, 15,* 666-681.

Tichy, N. M., & Devanna, M. A. (1986). *The transformational leader.* New York: John Wiley.

Toffler, B. (1986). *Tough choices: Managers talk ethics.* New York: John Wiley.

Triandis, H. C. (1984). Toward a psychological theory of economic growth. *International Journal of Psychology, 19,* 79-95.

Triandis, H. C. (1988). Collectivism and development. In D. Sinha & H. S. R. Kao (Eds.), *Social values and development: Asian perspective* (pp. 285-303). New Delhi: Sage.

Triandis, H. C. (1993). The contingency model in cross-cultural perspective. In N. M. Chemers & R. Ayman (Eds.), *Leadership theory and research* (pp. 167-188). San Diego: Academic Press.

Triandis, H. C. (1994). Cross-cultural industrial and organizational psychology. In H. C. Triandis, M. D. Dunnette, & L. M. Hough (Eds.), *Handbook of industrial and organizational psychology* (2nd ed., Vol. 4, pp. 103-172). Palo Alto, CA: Consulting Psychologists Press.

Trompenaars, F. (1993). *Riding the waves of culture.* London: The Economist Press.

Tuan, Y. (1982). *Segmented worlds and self.* Minneapolis: University of Minnesota Press.

Viega, J. F., & Dechant, K. (1993). Fax poll: Altruism in corporate America. *Academy of Management Executive, 7*(3), 89-91.

Virmani, B. R., & Guptam, S. U. (1991). *Indian management.* New Delhi: Vision.

Vitz, P. C. (1994). *Psychology as religion: The cult of self-worship* (2nd ed.). Grand Rapids, MI: Eerdmans.

Vroom, V. H., & Yetton, E. W. (1973). *Leadership and decision making.* Pittsburgh, PA: University of Pittsburgh Press.

Walton, C. C. (1988). *The moral manager.* Cambridge, MA: Ballinger.

Watson, C. E. (1991). *Managing with integrity: Insights from America's C.E.O.s.* New York: Praeger.

Weber, M. (1958a). *The Protestant work ethic and the spirit of capitalism.* New York: Academic Press.

Weber, M. (1958b). *The religions of India: The sociology of Hinduism and Buddhism.* Glencoe, IL: Free Press.

Weber, M. (1968). *Economy and society* (Vols. 1-3, G. Roth & C. Wittich, Eds.). New York: Bedminster. (Original work published 1925)

Westley, F., & Mintzberg, H. (1988). Profiles of strategic vision: Levesque and Iacocca. In J. A. Conger & R. N. Kanungo (Eds.), *Charismatic leadership: The elusive factor in organizational effectiveness* (pp. 161-212). San Francisco: Jossey-Bass.

Whiting, J. W. M. (1960). Resource mediation and learning by identification. In I. Iscoe & H. W. Stevenson (Eds.), *Personality development in children* (pp. 112-126). Austin: University of Texas.

Wilner, A. R. (1984). *The spellbinders: Charismatic political leadership.* New Haven, CT: Yale University Press.

Wilson, E. (1978). *On human nature.* Cambridge, MA: Harvard University Press.

Winter, D. (1973). *The power motive.* New York: Free Press.

Worchel, S., Cooper, J., & Goethals, G. (1988). *Understanding social psychology.* Chicago: Dorsey.

Woycke, J. (1990). Managing political modernization: Charismatic leadership in the developing countries. In A. M. Jaeger & R. N. Kanungo (Eds.), *Management in developing countries* (pp. 275-286). London: Routledge.

Yukl, G. A. (1989). *Leadership in organizations.* Englewood Cliffs, NJ: Prentice Hall.

Zaleznik, A. (1977, May-June). Managers and leaders: Are they different? *Harvard Business Review,* pp. 67-78.

Zaleznik, A. (1990). The leadership gap. *Academy of Management Executive, 4*(1), 7-22.

Author Index

Subject Index

Achievement, 44-45, 49-50
Affiliation, 44-46
Altruism:
    and achievement, 44-45, 49-50
    and affiliation, 44-46
    and charismatic leadership, 41-44
    and egotistic behavior, 36-37, 39-40, 42-
       44, 50
    and empowerment, 43-44
    and leadership effectiveness, 43, 44-50
    and morality, 33-36, 38, 40-41
    and participative leadership, 44-50
    and power, 44-45, 47-49
    and social leadership, 44-46
    and socioculturalism, 78-86
    and spirituality, 38, 40-41
    and task leadership, 44-45, 47-50
    behavior, 39-41
    characteristics, 36-41
    defined, 37
    necessity of, 84-86, 104
    obstacles to, 76-84, 104
    purpose of, 37-38

Behavior. See Role behavior
Buddhism, 125

Charismatic leadership:
    and altruism, 41-44

    and empowerment, 31, 43-44
    and environment, 102-104
    and follower characteristics, 26-29
    and morality, 98-102
    and patience, 99-100
    and persistence, 100-101
    and perspective, 101
    and pride, 99
    and purpose, 98-99
    and role behavior, 22-26
    and socioculturalism, 29-30, 107, 116-
       123
    and spirituality, 58-60, 92-98, 105, 120,
       122-123
    and task context, 26-27
    effectiveness of, 26-30, 43
    influence process of, 30-31, 57-61
    model of, 25
    See also Transactional leadership; Trans-
      formational leadership
Christianity. See Judeo-Christianity
Confucianism, 125
Culturalism. See Socioculturalism

Effectiveness of leadership:
    and altruism, 43, 44-50
    and follower characteristics, 27-29
    and socioculturalism, 29-30, 107-117
    and task context, 26-27
    charismatic, 26-30, 43

147

About the Authors

Rabindra N. Kanungo joined McGill University's Faculty of Management in 1969. He teaches courses in social psychology, cross-cultural management, organizational behavior, consumer behavior, and human resource management. He also has conducted training seminars for various management groups. Previously, he taught at Dalhousie University and several universities in India. His areas of expertise are comparative studies of work attitudes, work motivation, and leadership. His current research projects include cross-national studies on work motivation and alienation and the application of leadership research in developing countries. He has over 100 refereed publications, appearing in journals such as *Psychological Bulletin, Academy of Management Review,* and *Journal of Applied Psychology,* and is author or editor of over a dozen books in the field of psychology and management, including *Affect and Memory* (1975, with S. Dutta), *Work Alienation* (1982), *Countries* (1990, with A. Jaeger, eds.), *Compensation: Effective Reward Management* (1992, with M. Mendonca), and *Work Motivation: Models for Developing Countries* (1994, with M. Mendonca, eds.). As a distinguished researcher in the field, he became a fellow of the Canadian Psychological Association in 1976. He is also the recipient of awards from the National Research Council (NRC), Canada Council, and Social Science and Humanities Research Council (SSHRC). In 1988, he was awarded the Faculty of Management Chair in Organizational Behavior. He has many affiliations with the business community and serves as an editorial consultant for several journals in Canada, the United States, and the United Kingdom.

Manuel Mendonca has been teaching courses in compensation management, managing organizational change, managerial negotiations, human resource management, employment, and organizational behavior in McGill's Faculty of Management and Department of Continuing Education since 1984. Before this, he taught at St. Xavier's College, University of Bombay, India. He holds a certificate in teaching in pedagogical methods in business education. His current research interests are in employee compensation and cross-cultural management. He has coauthored two books: *Compensation: Effective Reward Management* (1992, with R. N. Kanungo) and *Introduction to Organizational Behavior* (1994, with R. N. Kanungo) and is coeditor of *Work Motivation: Models for Developing Countries* (1994, with R. N. Kanungo). He has contributed to journals such as *California Management Review, Journal of Management Inquiry,* and *Psychology and Developing Societies.* His 15 years in supervisory and management positions in the petrochemical and electrical industries give him firsthand business experience. He has concentrated in the areas of personnel, industrial relations, and management development throughout his career.